MIND YOUR OWN BUSINESS

The final piece
to the financial
planning puzzle

BY STEVE LYNCH

"Every once in a blue moon
a financial genius comes along
that doesn't want to hoard his secrets,
he wants to share them.
Either he's completely out of his mind
or is a true humanitarian. Perhaps both.
One thing's for certain, you'll come away from
this book richer in so many ways."

"Most of the time people
aren't just a little wrong.
Most of the time they're absolutely,
positively, undeniably wrong.
Fortunately, it's never too late to
right a wrong."

… Stephen C. Lynch, CFP®

Book design by Gabriela Rivas
Photography by Eric Williams

www.stevelynchwealth.com

6605 Uptown Blvd NE, Ste 330
Albuquerque, NM 87110

LIBRARY OF CONGRESS
CATALOGING-IN-PUBLICATION DATA

ISBN: 978-0-578-92854-8

Lynch, Steve
Mind your own business, nonfiction/Steve Lynch

For all who think big, start small—

this book is dedicated to you.

CONTENTS

STEVE LYNCH

ONE
BECOMING RICH

Let me begin by saying it's not as difficult as it may seem. There are countless ways of getting rich.

Some say, "Hey, man—start a bank!"

Others say, "Hey, dawg—rob a bank!"

And still others might say, "Yo, bro—invent the next whatsit!"

Well, know what I say?

I say go with the most common and reliable way to get rich!

What's that, you say?

Read on.

Granted, we can't all sing like Bowie or Adele. Nor can we all return a blazing serve like Djokovic. Or, for that matter, make a gangster flick like Scorsese. But there is one thing we *all* have in common and it's something *everyone* can do. We *all* can become rich.

And guess what? I, Steve Lynch, CERTIFIED FINANCIAL PLANNER™ professional, have honed a cool little *plan*.

Simply read on.

* * *

STEVE LYNCH

TWO

SCAMS, SCHEMES AND STINGS

It's not my wish to scare you straight. Scaring tactics worked great in the Army. Kept many a soldier from poking his head from out of a foxhole at the wrong time, or stepping carelessly across a minefield. As sounds go, I prefer *ka-ching* to *KA-BOOM!* But using scare tactics in business cramps my style. Nonetheless, you need to hear the truth. So here it is:

Life sucks if you don't have enough money. Also, without enough money, many a relationship is doomed.

Of course, I'm taking a broad view here, but if you're not going places, on the road to riches—or at least have a good map—nobody wants to hang around. Except, perhaps, a loyal dog.

But, if your future looks bright—

Well, you get the point.

And the point I generally try to make with everyone is to put at least $50 a month into an investment portfolio.

Anyways, I'm so determined to help others invest in themselves, I even read a book on conmen. The book said conmen tell you what you want to hear. (It would be nice if dentists did, too. Like "Steve, you've got zero cavities!" even when I don't. I brush, gargle and floss, but find it difficult to avoid a frozen Milky Way or three.)

A flourishing con artist combines psychology and charm (and a little magic) to identify the right mark, concoct the best ruse and, of uppermost importance, gain their victim's confidence. After all, that's why they are called confidence men.

Investment scams promise high returns without financial risk. But there's no such animal.

Most of you have seen the film *Guys and Dolls*, yes? (If not, what are you waiting for?) There's a marvelous quote in it written by the great Damon Runyon. The gambler/con artist Sky Masterson (played by Marlon Brando) says, "One of these days in your travels, a guy is going to show you a brand-new deck of cards on which the seal is not yet broken. Then this guy is going to offer to bet you that he can make the Jack of Spades jump out of this brand-new deck of cards and squirt cider in your ear. But, son, do not accept this bet, because as sure as you stand there, you're going to wind up with an earful of cider."

Well, let's say someone who seems legit informs you that you're related to the royal family, or have inherited a vast fortune, or some such cock and bull story, but you have to give them a small up-front payment, which the con artist requires, of course, in order to obtain the, uhm, humongous sum. And the con artist is very convincing, so you're thinking, "Oh boy! I won't ever have to work again!"

This is just the tip of the ol' iceberg lettuce, folks. There are countless get-rich-schemes out there and most every single one is fraudulent. Fake franchises, real estate "sure things," wealth-building seminars, foreign exchange fraud, Nigerian money scams, pyramid schemes, and of course, the ultimate scheme, the Ponzi sting. Bernie Madoff, the ultimate trickster, duped some of the coolest celebs in Hollywood. Like Keifer Sutherland, Robert De Niro, Anne Hathaway, Kevin Bacon, Uma Thurman and the coolest of all, Jack Nicholson. I guess you could say they all wound up with "an earful of cider."

The reason many conmen don't get caught (like Mr. Madoff did) is because the people that got tricked don't want to tell anyone that they fell for the scam.

Nobody wants to look like a dummy. So this shit keeps on going, and going, and going like that pink drum-pounding bunny, when, of course, we should be pummeling bad guys. Like that dog McGruff, take a bite out of crime. (Sorry for milking the anthropomorphic icon examples.)

But here's the rub (as that famous Prince of Denmark once said), people work their asses off all their lives and yet don't find themselves prepared for their "trophy years" a.k.a. retirement a.k.a. those (relaxing on a hammock in the shade of palm trees, listening to the waves, sipping mai tais) golden years. But do they confess to their financial stumbles? Warn the young? Hell, no. Because like those celebrated hoodwinked dupes (still wiping cider from their ears), owning up to not having a financial plan would make them look like... well, like dopes.

Hence, I wrote this book for you hoping to rid the

world of dupes and dopes. And authors who use the word "hence."

* * *

MIND YOUR OWN BUSINESS

STEVE LYNCH

THREE

THINK OF EACH DOLLAR AS A WORKER

And you're the boss.

You can start off with a few workers and pretty soon you have many.

Unless, of course, you fritter away those workers.

Of course, these metaphorical workers—a.k.a. *dollars*—come and go because, after all, we all have to eat, pay the bills, buy the latest doodad, and so forth and so on, ad nauseam. But if your allotted dollars are doing their job—working their little green buttocks off (for *you*)— then hopefully your personal little workforce grows and grows—more workers beget more dollars—and is not so "little" any longer, and, subsequently, the richer and richer (and *richer*) you can become. (I just love stories with a happy ending.)

But that might be getting a tad ahead of ourselves.

* * *

STEVE LYNCH

FOUR

WHAT IN BLAZES DOES IT MEAN TO BE RICH?

And by "rich" we're not talking fatty, oily or sweet. We're talking moneyed.

Everyone perceives rich differently.

As Sly and the Family Stone once sang, "Different strokes for different folks, and so on and so on, and scooby dooby doo."

For example, let's say you're Scrooge McDuck. According to Disney, you're worth "one multiplujillion, nine obsquatumatillion, six hundred twenty-three dollars and sixty-two cents". Being a rich duck also means wearing a frock coat, top hat, pince-nez glasses, and spats and having a huge Money Bin that overlooks the city of Duckberg. Don't worry, I haven't gone quackers (at least, not yet), just drawing a comparative picture how the perception of being rich differs from person to person, and duck to duck.

Okay, if being a duck ain't your cup of soup, then let's say you're a well-heeled pirate. You might have a solid gold peg leg and a treasure chest spilling over with silver coins and precious gems—so overflowing with booty, you can't get the stupid lid closed. Of course, any rich pirate worth his salt and having sailed The Seven Seas, plundering and pillaging and whatnot, would make sure his treasure chest was a size XXXL. And maybe if he was a sensible pirate, he brought along a CERTIFIED FINANCIAL PLANNER™ professional—one who didn't easily get seasick.

We'll get to that part of the book shortly. No, not the treasure chest part, the CFP® professional part. Because it would truly suck to be an *impoverished* pirate and have your brigantine repossessed.

Not to digress, but I have.

We were talking about how people perceive being "rich" differently. Maybe to you, it simply means being well-off. You know, like having enough dough so you'll never need to worry about *not* having enough dough. Having life's creature comforts. Like owning a home— or three. Or maybe, finally, at long last, getting that badass pickup truck. Or, if you're the seafaring type, have your very own customized brigantine. Although if the United States Coast Guard is nearby, I highly advise against flying the Jolly Roger.

In other words, "rich" is being *financially free* to do as you please, live as you please, do whatever the hell you want—within the confines of the law, of course.

Travel from here to Timbuktu and back again. As often as you like. Although you'd think one time would be enough. (And take heed: it's damn hard to find a decent pastrami sandwich anywhere south of the Niger

River.)

Oh, hell—being "rich" is so many different things to so many different people.

To some, it's simply having pockets deep enough to kick back in your hammock in your resplendent backyard listening to a ballgame or Mötley Crüe.

* * *

STEVE LYNCH

FIVE
RISKY BUSINESS

And by risky business, we're not talkin' about Tom Cruise dancin' in his tighty-whiteys to "Old Time Rock and Roll." We're talkin' about taking the less risky route to wealth.

Throughout the ages—from Pythagoras (a pithy pescatarian, or so I'm told) to Stiglitz (a Nobel-winning economist who likes kosher dill pickles, or so I'm once again told)—natural human behavior is to lower exposure to uncertainty. In other words, it's natural to avoid risk.

See saber-toothed tiger? Run, Ogg, run!

This holds true in almost all human endeavors. Uncertainty is perceived as risky. I knew a guy who once bet on Buster Douglas, a 42-1 underdog, when he took on an undefeated Mike Tyson. It was an uncertain bet to say the least, but he wasn't clairvoyant, just plain lucky. Sometimes even the stupid can get away with being stupid. Risk aversion, however, is not only a natural human trait but also one that is, perhaps, as important to our survival as knowing to unplug a toaster before sticking a fork in it.

The good news is, the most common way to get rich is the least risky.

Oh, don't get me wrong, there are many ways to strike it rich. The majority, though, is not nearly as reliable. It's cool to be an inventor, for sure. Or throw a baseball a 100 mph. Both can make you millions. But there are a scant number of inventions that succeed, and even fewer arms that can hurl major league heat.

Yes, there are inventions that make millions. But how many millionaires made their millions being inventors? I'd guess only about one percent. Barely. The other ninety-nine percent probably used a method we'll be getting around to shortly. But, once upon a mullet, when I was wet behind the ears (and, most likely, under the arms—I worked hard on construction sites), I daydreamed of one day becoming super rich by inventing something really cool. But instead of, let's say, a Slinky® or The Snuggie® or The Dogbrella™, I came up with a real humdinger. What I find to be a most reliable, straightforward way to get rich.

Ready? Okay, here's Step One: *Help others.*

(Sort of like what I'm trying to do by writing this book.)

I'm not necessarily saying join the Red Cross or volunteer for the Peace Corps, although both are noble altruistic occupations. I'm simply saying whatever your business is, in some way, it should help others. Do that and I think you might find you hit the mother lode. Because the more you help others, the richer you may get.

Yes, a boy scout helping old Maude Frickert cross the road is doing good—but so is being a plumber, a welder, a lumberjack, a hairdresser, a proctologist and so on and so forth. So many people make the big mistake of thinking the road to riches requires reinventing the light bulb, or winning the lottery, or starting a rock band, or selling socks in threes.

When we look at the wealthy, we discover that the vast majority followed Step One. They all had a person or a thingamajig that helped others. Then they most likely added a profit to that person or thingamajig. And a million "helps" later, figuratively speaking, they were millionaires. A darn good reason why a business should try to hire as many workers as is practical. After all, the name of the game is making the most amount of money with the least amount of risk.

* * *

STEVE LYNCH

SIX

NOTHING TO FEAR BUT F-F-FEAR ITSELF

Just remember there are two sides to every story. The Positive Side and the Negative Side. The Good Side and The Bad Side. The Upside and The Downside. The East Side and The West Side. (The latter being a damn good Broadway show, if you're into musicals.)

Now what I want to focus on is Loss and Gain. (And no, I'm not talking about the downside of a yoyo diet.) After spending the last couple decades trying to learn as much as I can about Behavioral Finance (or, as I prefer to call it, Behavioral Economics) it became crystal clear that Loss has a far greater effect on us humans. And, if you watch TV—and who doesn't except maybe goldfish—the gains (i.e., The Good Side) get very little ad time. Just remember how a con artist works: he/she tells us what we want to hear. So these ads are all about not losing money or, supposedly, paying debt down. In other words, they focus on the downside. Fear, fear, fear! Are these advertisers bad people? Of course not! They're just telling you what you want to hear. It takes two to tango. Right? (It also takes two to tickle—but that's another story.)

Now that I have brought this to your attention, is this good Economic Behavior? That's an excellent question, Steve, even if I say so myself. But the real question is what behavior makes you more money and brings you more happiness? Well, in the short-term, saving or "loss protection" probably wins out. But in the long-term, concentrating on gains is a win, win, win. So if you had an hour of energy, I would probably spend a good 70% of it—yes, you guessed it (I hope)—

on winning, winning, winning, which is, of course, gains, and making money, money, money. Now, why is the opposite so common and widespread? If I said f-f-fear (which stops people in their tracks from ever starting) I would probably be right. But again, this is short-term behavior and not very good behavior. But, in fact, it's not all mental. It's simply because there are a lot of very good people that just do not have very good Economic Behaviors. But, it's quite simple to fix. Simply hire somebody. Now maybe the first person you meet is not the right fit. What you need is someone with the knowledge and, more importantly, someone who likes to learn. (But beware of somebody you may like too much—because, oft times, that's the modus operandi of a con man.)

But getting back to the point, multiply your presence! I hire people to help with just about everything. I simply cannot have an almost perfect life (i.e., medical care, automobile, house, tennis racquets, and so forth) without the help of a lot of real good people. The power of economics.

The upshot is this: if you spend 90% of your time and energy on not losing, it's like the hamster on the wheel—work your tail off to get nowhere. A tragedy. One that can be prevented. Why do everything when there are experts in everything? It's how one multiplies their presence.

Sure, working hard is great. But wouldn't life be a lot easier (not to mention more rewarding) if you had a lot of workers? And by that I mean *dollars* all over the planet working for you, too?

* * *

STEVE LYNCH

SEVEN

STEVE 101
A fun little History Class

You already know my name. (In case you forgot, it's
on the cover of this book.) Perhaps you also don't
know this, but the way I help others is by being a
Certified Financial Planner™ professional. Or CFP®
professional, if you're into initialism. So how does a
CFP® professional help others? I like to explain it
thusly: every major corporation has a Chief Financial
Officer (or, for all you initialistic readers, CFO) whose
responsibility is to make all the company's financial
stuff right as rain. Well, I strive to do the same — but
for individuals, couples and small businesses. (Basically,

I help you "mind your business"—which is what this handy little book is about.)

General Motors likes to build Corvettes (and I'm glad they do), so they hire a bunch of financial virtuosos like me to help keep them out of trouble (or something like that). I was first introduced to Financial Planning in college, class of '82, back when Journey's "Don't Stop Believin'" was blasting on the radio, and I never stopped believin'. But back in the 60's and 70's, as I mentioned, I was lucky to be able to work in the construction business with my old man. Even before I hit my teens, I could make money in a puddle. When I was twelve growing up in Northwest Detroit, between 7 Mile and 8 Mile (I suppose you could say I grew up in 7½ Mile) I mowed lawns, shoveled walks, you name it, just to make a few bucks and to keep out of trouble. Oh yes, Mr. Lynch (my dear ol' dad) had his hands full with young Steve. Which is why he soon put me to work on a construction site. You might say I grew up on a job site swinging a hammer, pounding nails, and at that time they didn't have nail guns, they had me— Steve the Nail Gun—and I pounded, and I pounded, and I pounded, and I loved every minute of it. (It was also a helluva good excuse to hang around my dad.) So, my dad had paid me, and I took a shower, and I got ready, was going to go out, I was thirteen or fourteen, and I went up to my dad and I said, "Dad, can you loan me some money so I can go out tonight?" And he gave me a look as if a concrete beam had fallen on my head, rendering me brainless. "Son," he said, "I just paid you $34!" And I smiled and looked at him and said, "Yeah, dad, but I can't spend that. I gotta *save* that."

So I guess that's where it all began.

And yes, I also like to build stuff. But not just with two-by-fours like my dad. I "build" with dollars. Not to boast, but imagine my thirty-odd years of experience building wealth for my clients. Converting all their preconceived notions—even those who sell themselves short—and showing them that anyone—*everyone*—can be rich.

What is rich? That's for *you* to decide. Although as we get a little further along into this book, I will delve deeper into this question. But I'm not talking about a dark chocolate cake with a nice ganache glaze. (Even though as I write this paragraph I have a sudden case of the munchies). My goal is to get you to a phase where you can be a free thinker, not stressed out. Not worrying where the next buck is coming from. Not worrying about taking care of the parents and kids, taxes and the unforeseen. Personally, I love the journey. I love making people happy.

So, the punch line is: I'm writing this book because over thirty-plus years I think—no! I *know*—people are good. Except maybe "Stinky" Detweiller who sucker punched me back in the third grade. Then again, as the years passed, perhaps he's learned not only to practice better hygiene but maybe also kindlier ways. But, like I said, for the most part, people are fundamentally good. They work hard—some work *really* hard—they save (whatever they can), and try to do the right thing. So why isn't everyone rich? I ask myself the same question, which is why I wrote this book. Because, personally, I'd rather work with the numeral system than the alphabet. I'm dyslexic. Words, at times, look like hieroglyphics. In fact, just now, I had to ask my office manager, Jesus, how to spell dyslexic and hieroglyphics, and most other words, too—not counting cat, dog and dollars.

* * *

STEVE LYNCH

EIGHT
THE BUNDY CURSE

Everyone likes Al Bundy. Yes, you read that right. The one and only Al Bundy. The poor schnook on that old TV show *Married With Children* that ran in the '80s and 90's. The doofus with the lazy redheaded wife Peg, the principal contributor to The Bundy Curse. Al Bundy still, to this day, makes me laugh my butt off. He probably gave you a few laughs, too, but you certainly would not want to be Al Bundy, because Al Bundy, for want of a better word, is piss-poor. Or, if permitted to use numbers (which I'm best at) in lieu of words, he's a zero. A zilch. A zip. (If he were one of The

Marx Brothers, he'd be Zippo.)

What business is he in? The business of helping somebody *else's* business. And because it's not *his* shoe business, if Al doesn't go to work, he doesn't make any money. If he got hurt or had an emergency, he's strictly out of luck. And ol' Peg is a spendthrift extraordinaire. So in the Bundy family dollars do not linger long. I think Al and Peg would be much better off (though maybe not quite as funny) if they started to think and act like a BUSINESS. And, yes, you can think and act that way even if you're working for somebody else. That's the beauty of it!

I was in the army for a while. So here's the drill: I want you to think like a general, not like a private. A general has a lot of soldiers working for him, makes good money, too. A private has nobody working for him and makes way less money.

So, if you're counting, here's Step Two. (If you

recall, Step One was help others.) Step Two: think of yourself as a business.

Even if you're working for somebody else, *you're* the boss!

Now, think of every dollar as a worker. (Or, in the case of generals, every buck is a buck private.)

Look at it this way:

$1 =

$2 =

$3 =

And so it goes.

Every dollar equals a worker. So the idea is to put every dollar (a.k.a. worker) to work.

Every day you go to work. Every two weeks, perhaps, you get paid money. Bucks. Moolah. Shekels. Clams. Simoleons. Wampum. Dead presidents. Whatever you call it—and even though it seems like it's hardly ever enough—put those bucks, shekels, clams, simoleons (etc.) to work.

Picture each and every dollar a worker—working for *you*. That's how the rich think. And if you don't waste them—the dollars—they can *continue* to work for you. Forever and ever, and ever and ever.

But, if you give them away, spend them ill-advisedly, they will never work for you again. Such a stupidly simple concept! You give away your workers, then you will not be rich. You'll be the complete opposite of rich. And you know what that means. You'll be "Al Bundy poor."

So you don't have to start your own business. Just run your affairs like one.

As Humphrey Bogart said at the end of *Casablanca*, "Money, this is the beginning of a beautiful friendship."

Okay, in actuality, he said "Louie" not "money" but how do we know that Louie wasn't a pet name

Bogey used for money? But, either way, yes—this *is* the beginning of a beautiful friendship with money.

* * *

STEVE LYNCH

NINE

THINK BIG, START SMALL

Once upon a cold frosty beer, instead of pissing away fifty bucks each and every month, as he was prone to do, my ol' childhood pal Jimmy surprised just about everyone (except me, of course) when he decided, once and for all, to invest that fifty bucks into an investment portfolio.

But I'm getting a wee bit ahead of myself.

Remember what I said about helping others and how it's the right step toward building wealth?

Hold that thought as we flashback to 1991.

I had just returned from Operation Desert Shield

and was getting my financial planning business up and running again and decided to make a call to a friend—someone I've known since childhood.

My ol' pal Jimmy, at the time, was thirty-something and married with kids—much the same as Al Bundy. "I want you to do something—" I told him, pausing to take a sip of the cold frosty beer—"starting right now."

"Spit it out, good buddy," he said, quaffing a cold brew on his side of the call.

"Okay, but let me preface by saying if you don't do it, not only will you suffer long-term consequences but I will also come over there and give you a swift kick in the butt."

Maybe those weren't my exact words, but you get the gist.

In that brief call, I gave him some very sound financial advice.

"Listen," I said, "it's ridiculously simple: think big, start small."

I then went on to tell him (not unlike a Mr. Rogers—that's if Mr. Rogers cussed a lot) how a simple monthly plan, no matter how small, could result in his becoming fairly well-heeled.

Being one of my more good-natured friends, Jimmy said, "Geez, Steve, you make it sound so effing simple but I know, after knowing you all these many years, you wouldn't give your ol' buddy the bum steer. So, okay—I will do fifty bucks a month."

And that little call would change both his life and mine, forever.

No financial planner can promise you that you'll get the same results as someone else. That said, Jimmy's account, as of February 11th, 2022, is around $319,000[1A]. And that's *after* helping his oldest son with college.

Some might say they do this in their retirement plan. Yes, it's called "dollar cost average." Well, what I'm saying is everybody should be taking advantage what many others are doing *without* the restriction and penalties of a retirement plan.[1B]

Sometimes I like to tease him and say, "Hey, Jimbo, imagine if you had invested a *hundred* bucks a month! Or *five* hundred? Or five *thousand?*

Then I quickly duck, as an empty beer bottle sails past my head.

* * *

[1A] This case study is intended for illustrative purposes only. It may not be an appropriate strategy for, and does not necessarily reflect the potential experience of any other person. Individual needs vary and require consideration of each person's unique objectives and financial situation. Investing involves risk, and there is no guarantee of future performance or success.

[1B] Dollar Cost Averaging cannot eliminate the risk of fluctuating prices and uncertain returns, and cannot ensure a profit or protect against a loss and is subject to the investor's ability to continue purchases over periods of fluctuating markets. The discontinuance of the purchase of the security prior to the completion of the plan may detract from the benefits otherwise derived from Dollar Cost Averaging.

STEVE LYNCH

TEN
YE OLDE SAYINGS

There's this book I read many, many years ago. Uh-huh, I read a book. Ha ha. Actually, I read lots of books. I love books. And this particular book made quite an impression. If memory serves me well, it was titled *Gold Is In Your Backyard, Knucklehead*—I added the knucklehead part because that's what I was at the time—and it taught me, at a very young age, that gold is not necessarily in "them thar hills" but is right there under your schnozzola. Where am I going with this? Simply this: to become rich, you don't need to win the lotto. Or invent the light bulb. Or throw a football.

Or casually return a 150 mph serve. Or croon like Sinatra. The fact is, there's only a very small percentage of people who made their money that way. The most common way to create (and sustain) wealth is by thinking and acting like YOU ARE A BUSINESS.

As a rule, it's been making people rich since time immemorial.

At my office I joke about a helicopter that could take me to Western Turkey fifteen hundred years in the past to find the richest family and how they'd be business-minded people. And the path to wealth is the same today as it was back in 500 A.D. (In today's world we have a far greater selection of footwear, but even so, back then they could make a really awesome sandal.)

No matter how far back you go—whether you traveled in some imagined helicopter or through the pages of old books—you'll find many a wise philosopher. Some of their adages I am sharing with you. In the event, here or there, whenever a word sounded archaic or outdated, I may have replaced it with a word that's more contemporary. Like, for example, instead of a "thou" in its place I substituted a *you*. Instead of saying "behoof" I probably will say *benefit*. Instead of a "nay" it's a *no*. Forget the antiquated word "thither," I'll simply say to. And when it comes to a "gadzooks" or an "egads," I'll probably replace it with a *holy shit* or a *great googamooga!* Thou gets me drift. Oops, I mean, *you* get my drift.

Now don't go slamming this book shut and throwing it across the room because you think I'm going to be talking about a lot of old fogeys—most of whom are dead fogeys—many with long gray beards. Because even though they may have worn a toga or a codpiece, they sure as hell knew what they were talking about. And why you should take care of your money as if it's a business and you're the boss.

A lot of the wise old sayings are attributed to some Greek fella named Aesop. For example, here, in his own words, is the moral of his famous fable *The Tortoise and The Hare*— translated from choliambic verse, also known as limping iambs, scazons or halting iambi (which clears up the etymology of the idiom "It's all Greek to me"): *Up and be doing is an edifying text; for action is the business of life, and there's no thought of ever coming to the end of our journey in time, if we sleep by the way.*

Or, to make it *less* Greek for you:

You snooze, you lose.

Or, to put it yet another way:

Slow and steady wins the race. (And, for the most part, the riches.) Because every great financial plan requires a modicum of stick-to-itiveness.

Okay, here's another cool old saying:

A journey of a thousand miles begins with a single step.

Or, in Jimmy's case:

A journey of three hundred thousand smackeroos begins with a mere fifty bucks.

Of course, it's obvious this is an old Chinese proverb thousands of years old because today we would most likely begin a journey of a thousand miles in something a bit more swift than sandals. Like in Nikes. Or in a sleek Corvette Stingray. (The latter would be my choice, unless, of course, the wifey and kids wanted to tag along—in which case the journey would begin in a van.)

Anyways, where was I?

Oh yeah, right—this ancient proverb about a long journey beginning with a single step. It's attributed to Confucius, although some have credited another Chinese wise guy named Laozi— pronounced Lousy (which is probably how Confucius felt when somebody told him some other guy said these words before he did). But whoever said it, it's as true today as it was back then. Especially when it comes to financial planning, as Jimmy so gleefully found out:

Think big, start small.

Another adage I'm quite fond of is:

He who laughs last laughs best.

Or:

He who laughs last probably didn't get the joke.

As is the case with most of my stupid one-liners.

But it's no joke. Because someone who is not right away successful but has a smart financial plan can ultimately succeed where many other get-rich-quick pathways failed. It's a truism I can vouch for, having been a financial planner for thirty-odd years. Some years odder than others.

Further along in this "brilliant book" (said nobody, uh, yet) we'll talk about one of my favorite transcendentalist thinkers and his principle of *multiplying your presence*. But, for now, 'tis only fitting (notice how I cunningly tossed in a '*tis* being that the topic is bygone sayings?) we conclude this little chapter with these words of wisdom:

Everyone can be rich—for there is no shortage of money.

Who said that, you ask?

'Tis *I* that said that.

* * *

STEVE LYNCH

ELEVEN

HOW UNCLE SAM HANDLES DEBT.

A most excellent lesson.

Mark Twain— yes, that witty Huckleberry guy with the walrus moustache—once said (or maybe *twice* said): "It ain't what you don't know that gets you in trouble. It's what you know for sure that just ain't so."

Now if you're as brilliant as Mark Twain, you can get away with saying *ain't*. The meaning of that Twain observation is simple yet brilliant: It isn't (or, should I say, *ain't*) a lack of knowledge that gets you into trouble. It's false knowledge that gets you into trouble.

Being a CFP® professional, I've pulled more than a few troubled souls out of proverbial hot water.

Debt, like cement shoes, can sink you fast.

For some, debt is too emotional of a topic to discuss. Yet it's perhaps the most monumental impediment to becoming rich.

Or so people would like to think.

So people work their butts off to pay off debt because everybody just assumes that's how it works. No questions. Well, call me one of the idiots that did question it.

Like I said, some think it's way too hot of a subject to talk about. It's been known to get people's blood boiling or their eyes crossing—or both. In some cases, steam shoots out from their ears like in a Yosemite Sam cartoon. Nobody on TV talks about it. They prefer to talk about the widget—that is to say, the stupid investment.

My mother would tell us a story about her redneck in-laws (my father's side of the family). My great grandfather, who was born in the heat of the Civil War, once saw my mom wearing a bathing suit. This was shortly after WWII, mind you, and swimwear was a far cry from the micro bikinis we see today and, needless to say, couldn't care less about. But to my great grandpa, the sight of a woman's bare legs and shoulders was downright scandalous and he had such a conniption he reached for a stick to give my mom a backwoods whuppin'.

But I digress.

The story my mother would tell was about how my great granddad was a sharecropper and did so well that the property-owner made him an attractive proposition. "Bill," he said to my great grandpa, "if you bought the land and paid me what you are paying me now, within a few years you would own the land, outright."

"Hell, no," my great grandpa said. "I will neveh owe nobody nothin'."

Today that sounds positively idiotic. But before you rush to judge my great grandpa, he was very influenced by the early 1800's when they still had debtors' prisons and if you didn't pay your debts you suffered the severe consequences. Charles Dickens' family, for example, ended up in debtors' prison in 1824, under the Insolvent Debtors Act of 1813, because—now get this—he owed some baker £40 and 10 shillings. Back in 1824, that might've been a lot of pork pie but certainly no reason to toss a family into the pokey.

Thanks to "Chuck" Dickens (I like to imagine he and I would've been close chums) and also government economists, no longer are people imprisoned simply for trying to start a business. Now, they can file for bankruptcy. No longer is it a stigma. In fact, a certain famous former head of state declared bankruptcy a half dozen times. We live in a country that wants people to keep trying! If at first you don't succeed, etc., etc.

Now let's talk about how the U.S handles its debt.

Does anyone believe the government is trying to pay off its debt?

Naturally, whenever I pose that question people laugh. Then I ask, "Do you think they're stupid?" And, of course, the answer is no. (At least more often than naught.) They understand economics.

Do you know that our debt actually helps the world economy?

Question: Where does the world put their yen, yuan, pounds sterling, francs, centavos and euros to be safe?

Answer: U.S. Treasury bonds.

So the government borrows at two percent (although I'd bet cheaper). This sounds like how banks do it, right? Well, guess what? That's how all businesses do it. In fact, is anybody really in business if they aren't doing it? Emerson called it Multiplying Your Presence. It's business. It's beautiful. Government and business are using it to get rich. It's why Americans rarely lack products.

Now, maybe you don't have enough purchasing power. Maybe you're working your butt off trying to get out of debt.

Well, that's why I wrote this book.

* * *

MIND YOUR OWN BUSINESS

STEVE LYNCH

TWELVE
WHERE'S WALDO?

Before I answer that question, answer me this:

Where do people go wrong?

Maybe you saw that hilarious Mel Brooks movie *The Producers*. If so, perhaps you also recall, near the end, when their Broadway-bound show—the one these two scoundrels were hoping would be a titanic flop so they could swindle their investors—is suddenly a phenomenal success. A rousing success in spite of the fact that they did everything they could to fail. "How could this happen?" moaned producer Max Bialystock. "I was so careful. I picked the wrong play, the wrong director, the wrong cast! Where did I go *RIGHT?*"

But the question, in actuality, is: *Where do people go wrong when they try so hard to be right?*

To reiterate a Mark Twain quote: "It ain't what you don't know that gets you in trouble. It's what you know for sure that just ain't so."

I think we all suffer a little from that malady. Thinking we know something when in actuality we don't know diddlysquat. We all know how to crack an egg. Scramble an egg. But that doesn't mean we can all bake a soufflé. We need the pastry chef. Or, at least, the recipe. Which is why it's of my belief that life is a hell of a lot easier when you know what you want. And you have a *plan*. And, if you're really smart, a planner! (Especially one whose first name is Steve and last name rhymes with cinch.)

Which brings us once again to one of my favorite transcendentalist thinkers, the guy I promised we'd get back to in a prior chapter. Ralph Waldo—not to be confused with Ralph *Lauren* or Ralph *Kramden*—Emerson!

The ol' professor was a fervent believer in the power of the individual. Which is why he said: "Look to multiplying your presence."

It's a proven principle that has made many an individual a wealthier individual.

"It is best to pay for a skillful gardener," Emerson said, "or a sailor with a good sense of navigation [because by doing so] you multiply your presence [and by applying this good sense to your account and personal affairs] spread yourself throughout your estate."

Cool dude, that Waldo.

He goes on to say: "Do the thing, and you shall have the Power."

And he's not talking about doing steroids or

running for president. He's simply talking about having a fundamental advantage in the pursuit of happiness. And pursuit of wealth.

People (and we're talking mostly guys) wake up in the morning and say, "Zowie! I have it all figured out. If I save $100 then I am $100 smarter." So they go through life looking for opportunities to be cheap. Or, as Ralph Waldo Emerson would say, a less skilled gardener or an *inexperienced* sailor, et cetera.

Well, it's not simply about cutting costs and corners. To explain the principal of multiplying your presence, Emerson used the example of working on a farm.

Let's say, working on the farm, you can produce 10 units of work a day.

So theoretically, if you hire one more worker it's 1+1 = 2.

Or, keeping with this example, 10 units of work

plus 10 units of work equals 20 units of work.

Right? Makes perfect sense, does it not?

Well, guess what? Emerson got a different result!

He said we produced 30 units of work, not 20.

Because, by working together, everything got easier!

This is economics! It's also human capital, which is

the combination of skills, knowledge and experience

possessed by an individual viewed in terms of their

value to a company. Or, in this example, a farm.

Most will not hire because all they see are the

costs, not the value.

They think, *Hmm, if I hire somebody that's $20
an hour, and I'm smart enough to figure out that $20/
hour times 8 hours = $160 a day times 5 days = $800 a
week times 4 weeks = $3,200 a month times 12 months =
$38,400 times 10 years = $384,000 ... times, times, times
...* well, you get the idea. Under *this* kind of thinking,

nobody would ever have a job!

Which means it's absolutely *false* thinking.

The saying goes, "It is very easy to figure out the cost of everything but very tough to figure out the value."

Take, for example, W. Edwards Deming.

Even though he didn't grow up in a badass neighborhood like I did, he was, nonetheless, a real badass. In fact, there's an award for quality and efficiency named after him. The Deming Prize. And here's why. This guy Deming, back in the 1960's, goes to Detroit (yes, the same rough hood where I sprung from) and he says to the powers that be, "I can show you how to be a more efficient auto company." Well, it just so happens that at that time the auto companies were making money hand over fist and said, "Beat it, bud!" Or something to that effect.

So Deming ends up in Japan. And the rest, as they say, is history.

You see, at the time, The Motor City saw something like 15,000 vehicles roll off its production lines every day. To achieve that goal, the line workers were being measured on velocity, often at the expense of quality. At the same time, Japanese auto workers were applying economical methods learned from W. Edwards Deming and implementing new supply chain management practices enabling them to manufacture a higher quality vehicle, for less cost—and also at a higher velocity. As a result of Japan applying Deming's methods, they gained a 20% share of the U.S. auto market. Proving, once again, Mark Twain's certainty that "It ain't what you don't know that gets you in trouble. It's what you know for sure that just ain't so." Also, once again confirming Ralph Waldo Emerson's theory of "multiplying your presence."

Mr. Deming said something I found very interesting. He said people don't go to work to mess up, they go to do a good job. Wow! You mean everyone's out there working hard trying to do good things? That certainly shines a different light on the stock market, does it not? Emotionally, we say it can't work. Then we look at the long-term track record of the market and/or mankind's process (the two are one and the same), and we realize how far we have advanced.

Think of Bill Gates. How many people work for him? I would think thousands. Actually, when he resigned as Chairman and CEO of Microsoft back in 2008 (to start The Bill & Melinda Gates Foundation), the Microsoft Corporation employed over 128,000 people worldwide. (Talk about multiplying your presence!) And yes, he made a lot of money. (And "a lot" is a pretty big number.)

Now, for comparison's sake, think of Al Bundy, one of TV's saddest yet funniest characters. How many worked for Al Bundy? Zero. It was just Al and Al alone. If he doesn't go to work, he doesn't make money.

Bill Gates doesn't go to work and he still makes a shitload. Now Bill, or any other businessman, could not survive unless their employees PAID FOR THEMSELVES! A wake up call, yes?

So, instead of just calculating the cost, what if you started to think like a businessman. You would certainly start thinking differently. You would think to yourself (like a businessman): "If I hire somebody, they will pay for themselves! They will multiply my presence! I don't pay for them, they pay for themselves! Holy shit!" Then, hopefully, for your own sake, you will take the thought even further: "If I hire a Financial Planner, he will pay for himself? HOLY SHIT!"

Now you may think I'm doing all the Financial Planners a favor, right? Actually, I'm doing all the Al Bundys a favor. A great big enormous favor. I'm telling all the Al Bundys of the world that they—the hard workers—need to make their little workers (a.k.a. dollars) work hard, too.

And once they do—whoa! It's a life changer.

* * *

STEVE LYNCH

THIRTEEN

GRASPING THE STOCK MARKET

The stock market is all about multiplying your presence.

And you may not know this, but it's true: the whole stock market thing is designed for the *small* investor. Yes, a CFP® professional can open accounts for just about everyone. No matter how small the investment. Whether it's investing $50 a month (like Jimmy) or $500 a month. The small guy (Jimmy when first starting out) can build wealth (Jimmy *now*).

In fact, that's why my company's slogan is "Think Big, Start Small."

And when you think about it, just about everyone started small. In fact, I did a little research:

~ Oscar-winner Halle Berry slept in a homeless shelter when she first started her acting career.

~ Ed Sheeran, one of the biggest names in music (and if you don't believe me, ask my daughter) slept in subway stations on top of heating vents when he first started out.

~ Multi-billionaire Larry Ellison went from being an orphan to owning Oracle. His last name Ellison is a nod to Ellis Island.

~ Starbucks' CEO Howard Schultz grew up in the projects of Canarsie, Brooklyn, the son of a truck driver.

~ And, last but not least, the ancient Greek who invented the wheel couldn't afford a stonemason's hammer. Or so legend has it.

From rags to riches. Against all odds. Where there's a will, there's a way. Starting small, dreaming big.

And so it goes. It's not at all about being born with a mouthful of silver spoons.

And take it from a CFP® professional (with the initials SCL, he said with a wink), *thinking big, starting small* is one of the best ways to invest. Wait, did I say *one of* the best ways? I stand corrected, it's the best way (in my humble opinion).

"I don't like the market's ups and downs"

(And other misconceptions.)

Huh? Back when you were a little kid, didn't you like riding the seesaw? And how about the ups and downs of a trampoline? Well, kiddo, take it from Newton's Universal Law of Gravity, what goes up eventually comes down. Nothing in this universe is stagnant. Everything is moving. My house, for example, is moving every second. And I'm not living on the San Andreas Fault line, either. Granted, eventually, one day, it will settle. But if you think everything's stable just because nobody tells you otherwise, you'd be mistaken.

Everything is in motion. In fact, if someone tells you about an investment that doesn't move, run!

Saying "I want to invest in something that is, somehow, someway, not affected by the stock market" is another misconception. And you know what I say? "Ha! Good luck!" Value is based on supply and demand. Whether it's the price of crude oil, beer or toilet paper. Furthermore, when people don't have jobs they can't buy stuff, which, in turn, affects the value of my home. And so forth. But look at it this way: you still experience a downside whether you invest or not. But those who don't invest have all the downside but rarely any of the upside!

Here's an interesting statistic: According to author Mark Quinn (*Rich Man, Poor Bank*), immigrants are four times more likely to become millionaires than natural-born-citizens. Why is that? They came here from all over the world to fulfill the great American dream—the belief that you, regardless of where you were born or what class you were born into, can attain success in a society where upward mobility is possible for everyone. In fact, if you're poor, your chances of becoming rich are far greater than someone who isn't poor.

The opportunity to own stocks makes you a part owner of the company, because when you own shares you own a share of the company's assets and profits. In a lot of countries, owning a part of a company is just a fantasy. America is a powerhouse because everyone is free to invest in its companies.

A street named Wall.

Wall Street is a national treasure. One of the world's great inventions, right up there with fire, the wheel, electricity, penicillin, the Internet and the Frisbee. Its sole purpose is to allow small investors (regular guys and gals, like you and me) to be an important part of the whole shebang. To rise to the top of the food chain, so to speak—without having to be a great white shark or a Tyrannosaurus rex. Around two hundred and fifty years ago there was the king, and then everyone else. Now everybody can be a king. Or a queen. Or, in some cases, both.

Since this book is about making money, I have to impart a word or two (or two hundred) about resentment and rancor. That's right, jealousy—the green-eyed monster. Some folks don't like the stock market simply because it's in New York City.

"Damn Yankees!" says one.

"Only fools live above the Mason-Dixon Line!" says another.

And so on. And so forth.

But, in fact, Wall Street is not just IN New York, it's everywhere. The street called Wall is just where they keep score. Yes, in essence, it's just a scoreboard.

Thinking otherwise is thinking small.

Fact is, Wall Street was Wall Street even before there was a Wall Street.

Whoa! Let me rephrase that. Before the New York Stock Exchange and NASDAQ existed, there existed an eight-block-long street running northwest to southeast from Broadway to South Street, at the East River. The name of the street originates from an actual wall that the Dutch built in the 17th century, back when New York was called New Amsterdam. The Wall Street area became a center of trade in the 18th century but didn't become the street famous for being the financial center until 1792 when a couple dozen of the country's first and most illustrious brokers signed the Buttonwood Agreement, named after their customary meeting place under a buttonwood tree (don't worry, there's not going to be a pop quiz). The agreement became one of the most important financial documents in U.S. history. It outlined the common commission-based form of trading securities.

Even though Wall Street was, at first, synonymous for producing captains of industry like Rockefeller, Carnegie and Morgan, it was Middle America, the hoi polloi, the common folk "thinking big but starting small" that made the street named after a wall the epicenter of wealth that it is today, where everybody can be a captain.

Jealousy is stupid. Japan has been very successful not being stupid. And the kind of stupidity I'm talking about is the "if it's not my idea I will not use it" kind of stupidity. Japan is immune to that kind of stupid. If it's a good idea, then it's a good idea. They quickly start using the good idea and then improve upon it. It's intelligent behavior. It's also rich behavior. In Japan, you look smarter not dumber by standing on others' shoulders.

Do you have rich behavior? I hope so, because

there is no shortage of money.

* * *

FOURTEEN

WHY I WANTED TO BE A CFP® PROFESSIONAL

For the same reason, I suppose, that someone wants to be a doctor or a nurse, or a fireman or a teacher, I wanted to be a CFP® professional. Which is, to help others.

First, though, let me say I think I'm living proof that you don't have to be super smart to be successful. Because if there's something you can't figure out for yourself, there's someone who can figure it out for you. And all you have to do is be able to ask. That's why I became a CERTIFIED FINANCIAL PLANNER™ professional. I wanted to help others. As the transcendental philosopher Ralph Waldo Emerson so aptly put it (and it's one of my favorite Waldo-isms): *To be YOURSELF in a world that is constantly trying to make you something else is the greatest accomplishment.*

I think helping others is what life is all about. It's how you win in life. Be someone's hero. Sort of like what I'm trying to do with this book. (Emphasis on the word *trying*.)

Heroes are necessary. Not just first responders—who, in my book, are most definitely super heroes—but all kinds of heroes. The father who works two jobs so his kids can go to a better school. Or the guy or gal that brings hot meals to a homeless family. Or just being some guy whose job is making sure his clients never have to worry about when they get old and having enough to retire on so they can enjoy what should absolutely be their golden years.

Now we all know that being rich means

different things to different people. Some want to live in a penthouse while others might want to date a Penthouse "Pet." Some maybe want to jet to Paris for lunch and dinner in Majorca, while others might want to own the jet that flies you there. For many, it means having the resources to take care of oneself and family. But I also always wanted to make enough so I could help others. I'm sure just about everyone probably thinks like that. Maybe we all have different reasons for wanting to be rich, but I believe we all want to be heroic, in one way or another. There's a little Spider-Man or Spider-Woman in all of us, so to speak. Except, perhaps, if someone has arachnophobia, like Little Miss Muffet who sat on a tuffet (whatever *that* is). But I'm sure, in her Mother Goosey way, she, too, wanted to do stuff to help others. Maybe share her curds and whey (whatever the heck *that* is.)

So, at the risk of being redundant, one of the best things about my job is helping others. You see, my little brain (little in comparison to Einstein's, that is) needs to be engaged in some heroic mission, and that heroic mission is to make more people richer.

True, if you have enough resources to care for yourself, as well as others, and your mind is engaged—a fervent mind—I would say you are most definitely already rich and don't need to change a damn thing about yourself. Nonetheless, it's also nice to have lots of money.

So, yes, siree, Bob— it's time to become even richer.

* * *

FIFTEEN

NOT YOUR FAULT. WE'RE JUST NOT WIRED FOR THIS SHIT

I stumbled across an article, the purpose of which has nothing to do with building financial wealth but is so spot-on regarding humans' health. Then again, financial health and physical health are closely paired. Bear with me.

Laura L. Carstensen, professor of psychology at Stanford University and founding director of the Stanford Center on Longevity, said something astounding is happening. For most of human history, life expectancy was barely long enough to ensure survival of the species.

During the Roman Empire, life expectancy at birth was a paltry twenty-five years. (Who knows? Maybe quenching the blood thirst of Colosseum audiences might've contributed some to that low average life expectancy.) By the Middle Ages, life expectancy reached thirty-three years. (Although I'm thinking if not for the plague, average life expectancy might've been a wee bit higher.) As recently as the early 20th century, the average lifespan was fifty-five years—which today we look upon as still pretty low. (Heck, George Blanda, the great quarterback and place kicker, was nearly fifty when he retired.) Then, by the mid-twentieth century, a blink of an eye in evolution terms, Americans began flourishing into their eighties, nineties and beyond. (May we all be so fortunate to reach "beyond.")

Asked in a recent survey about the prospect of century-long lives, the majority of Americans said they would like to live to a hundred years if they could do so in good health. (And perhaps have enough zip left to rally with Andre Agassi. Is that asking too much?)

Of course, in the same New York Times survey nearly as many Americans said they eat way too much and lack exercise. (Unless if scampering to the fridge for another cold brew is considered exercise.) Hope is a wonderful thing, but hope alone will not get us to our hundredth birthday. After all, one must also have monetary longevity.

So, if you are the kind of person that lives for today, then historically you are the norm. But keep in mind, we are not programmed for long term financial success. I recently had a client turn a hundred. Good thing she had a financial plan because she now has the resources to live another hundred—or, at the very least, sustain her for years to come.

It's good to hope. It's even better to plan.

* * *

STEVE LYNCH

SIXTEEN

HOW TO DEAL WITH THE FINANCIAL SIDE OF LIFE.

Mark Twain sure as hell knew what he was talking about when he said, "It ain't what you don't know that gets you in trouble. It's what you know for sure that just ain't so."

Well, here's what I know for sure: K.I.S.S.

That's right: Keep It Simple, Stupid.

I do it with a simple analogy I've used my entire career: what a CFO does for corporations, a CFP® professional does for individuals.

Think of a CFP® as your family's (or small business') CFO. It's that simple.

General Motors wants to build Corvettes. But they don't want to deal with the financial side of it. Not at all. So, what do they do? They hire people like me to do that for them. GM may not "know for sure" what is or what ain't (as Mr. Twain would say) but their CFO knows. And it's so much easier when you get help from someone who knows.

It's why education is so important. My favorite form of education is traveling. Being in the army allowed me to travel around and meet so many different people. And excelling in sports helped me build confidence. So, playing tennis in college, then being exposed to so many different cultures in my travels, gave me the swagger to set my goals high. Why do you think those who came back from WWII—"The Greatest Generation"—were so successful? They said, "If someone else can do it, I sure as hell can do it, too." And they did! But you don't have to fight the bloody Axis in order to say this. We all can.

So, the question is: Can you become wealthy on a medium-sized income? And the answer is: Hell, yes! In fact, that was the starting point of most rich guys and gals.

Let's hope you don't wait too long to realize it.

* * *

SEVENTEEN

WHAT IF DEBT IS NOT YOUR PROBLEM?

What I see every day is extreme fear of debt. It's a phobia doctors call chrometophobia. (A cool name for a band? "Yo, give it up for Chrometophobia!)

This frightened, anxious behavior causes countries and people to underperform. Some never make it out of poverty. It's very sad. So I look at it from a different point-of-view. Debt can be good or bad, everyone knows that. Or at least I hope! House, college or business debt can be good. And I bet you know the debts that aren't so good.

Now, what if there was a debt thermometer!

119

Imagine, if you will, when your debt gets to a certain level—or "temperature"—would you race home and tell the wife or hubby to immediately stop buying stuff until the temperature is reduced? Okay, maybe. So then you work down the debt a few "degrees." At which point, one of two things can happen. One: an emergency. Or Two: you say you're not going to live like this—by "this" I mean poor—any longer. Either way, you spend money. And, either way, debt jumps right back up. This seesawing can go on for the rest of your life. You're caged in a psychological Debtors Prison! And feeling "feverish" most of the time.

If you recall, several chapters back, I told you about my father's side of the family and how in the early days of the 20th century my great grandpa was share cropping land, and whatever he produced, half of it went to the landowner. And how, one day, the landowner suggested that if my great grandpa were to buy the land, he could own it outright in a few years.

All of that makes perfectly good sense, right? Well, not to my great grandpa. The family's philosophy a hundred years ago was a lot different.

"Naaah!" he said, more than likely expectorating a pinch of chaw on the landlord's boot. "Neveh will I owe anybody anythin'—not a plug nickel!" Of course, I have no idea what he actually said, or whether he chewed tobacco or Wrigley's Spearmint. But I do know he wanted nothing to do with debt.

You must understand where he was coming from. Back then, if you borrowed money and couldn't afford to pay it back, off to debtors' prison you went, jiggity-jig.

Yup, like the ol' Monopoly card says: "Go directly to jail. Do not pass go. Do not collect $200." Back in the (not-so) good old days, when it came to deadbeats, the court of law weren't playing games.

If the great author Charles "Chuck" Dickens, let's

say, wrote a pamphlet on the principals of economics, not too many would read it. But, instead, he wrote *A Christmas Carol*, which is a splendid lesson in economics. That's because, as mentioned earlier, his family had been sent to debtors' prison. (Parliament, back then, wasn't exactly on theirs toes. Having a debtor's prison put the kibosh on many a bright idea. What a shame.) So you can imagine all the doubts and fears that were spinning around inside my great grandpa's noggin. He was living in an era that was a chrometophobic nightmare!

But what if debt is not your problem?

Yes, if you mishandle debt, it could kill you— figuratively speaking, of course. Fire can do the same thing (although fire does it literally), but does anybody quit using fire?

Okay, what I'm getting at is, there's much to gain in this chapter but you must be logical, not emotional.

Easier said than done, but let's try.

Be a master of debt, not a prisoner.

A debt master would obtain their debt somewhere with a favorable rate. We are now loaning money to qualified clients at 1.25 percent. How hard should you work to pay off a debt at 1.25 percent? The answer is, not very hard.

What you do is take all your present assets and put them to work for you. The best debt is an offense. Of course it is! Ask yourself how hard is the US government working at trying to pay off its debt? Hardly.

Are they stupid? No. Inflation eats away at the debt, given time. It's economics!

Is economics working *for* you or *against* you?

Even if you pay everything off, you're (more than likely) still paying out of the wazoo.

I had to get some work done on my truck's stereo

and the owner of the stereo shop asked if the truck was paid off.

I said no.

Actually, it was paid off, but I am still constantly paying for it: gas, tires, oil changes and all that jazz. Same as my home. Even if my home was paid off (which it is not) I am constantly pouring money into it.

Now let's return to my little analogy about every dollar being a worker. Stop giving away your workers. Let them work for you. With time, and a plan, you could have a million workers working for you.

Al Bundy has no workers. So, if he doesn't go to work, he makes no money. Think about it, ranchers have a lot of cows working for them. All businesses do the same. No, companies like Walmart don't have cows working for them. I was merely speaking metaphorically. But all companies borrow, build, produce and repeat. That's why I try to get my clients to act like they are a business. And to mind their business like they are the "president."

Now here's another interesting perspective. Some people think there's good debt and bad debt. Huh? Does this matter to the person that has the debt? Hell, no! They got debt. And that's that! Period. The question is, how to get out. The answer is the same: store debt at the lowest rate and start building wealth. Just like the USA does! Like I said, the best defense is a good offense. In laymen's terms: you can either use your "workers" to pay off a debt or you can keep your "workers" and invest them. Now, if you believe a dollar equals a worker, the more workers working, the more money you can make. And one day someone will ask you why you're glowing, and you can say that your wealth is growing. Or, if you're less poetic, simply reply, "*Ka-ching!*"

* * *

My childhood friends: Jimmy, Kenny and KT.
(Or, as I like to call them, "The Brain Trust.")

STEVE LYNCH

THINK BIG!

I love fishing but I always "catch and release."
Say hello to my little friend.

EIGHTEEN

INVESTORS VERSUS INVENTORS.

Back to my mother again, God bless her. As a kid, she would fill my head with grand stories about my grandfather. He was one hell of a guy. In the 1930's and 40's he was always trying to better himself. Went to night school and became an electrical engineer.

As my mom's story goes, my maternal grandfather decided to become an inventor. He came up with a thingamajig that turned off the sound on a TV so you didn't have to suffer through a lot of annoying commercials. Back then, if you wanted to silence a loathsome jingle or an irritating announcer's voice you had to lift your rump off the couch and lumber over to the TV and, using thumb and forefinger, turn the volume knob. (Yes, I know, sounds exhausting, right? Back in my Steve the Nail Gun days, I also served part-time as my dad's personal remote control device. Steve the Zapper.) The act of silencing the TV was a process that demanded physical activity which, in retrospect, was probably healthier than sitting there like a couch potato. My grandfather's remote muting device would change all that and make him a bundle. Or so he thought. But, as it turned out, he was up against the big boys—corporations like Zenith and Philco—the heavy hitters. (Zenith came out with a hand-held thumb-clicker fittingly called Lazy Bones, and Philco's widget was called Mystery Control.)

So, my point is, it's a crucial mistake to think that to become rich takes being an inventor or winning the lottery or becoming a steroidal athlete. Because if you took all the wealthy people in the world and, let's say, put them in a corral—yes, Tex, it would be a mighty big corral—what percentage of these millionaires do you think made their wealth by inventing some doohickey or hamming it up in some dumb movie or smacking a golf ball three trillion yards? If you said a very small percentage, you'd be spot-on. If you said barely one percent, you'd be exactamundo, as The Fonz would say. So who ended up wealthier? Some inventor like my grandpa or some investor?

But what if the plan and not your investment is the problem?

We now know, according to the 2021 Wealth-X World Ultra Wealth Report, that the vast majority of ultra-high net worth (UHNW) individuals—those worth at least $30 million—are self-made. 72%, to be exact. (Granted, that percentage is for the entire world, not just the United States—but America, after all, is the land of UHNW self-made millionaires.)

So maybe you think you should be "inventing" new, get-rich-quick investments for your portfolio? Wrong! You should be finding the best "long-term wealth-building" investment strategy. That's right! And build wealth the good old fashion boring way! But, take my word for it—or take Warren Buffett's—there's nothing boring whatsoever about getting rich.

Now, as for myself, I like boring well-diversified equities. When a person goes to college and works determinedly towards a Masters in Business Administration (an MBA, which is not to be confused with the NBA who, generally speaking, have a dramatic height advantage) the first twenty-six seconds of the two-year Master Degree Program is spent on educating us on what a widget is! A widget is a Corvette, toilet paper, Legos and whatnot. And, like I said, the professor would probably spend no more than twenty-six seconds on the topic. Twenty-eight, tops. The rest of the two-year Master's program is spent on how *business* works.

As a seasoned financial planner, how much time do I spend on widgets, i.e. the investments? Twenty-six seconds, perhaps. You see, amateurs are trying to get rich quick. Amateurs play the lotto. Most amateurs think it's all about the stupid investment. But the pros are trying to do it with the *least* amount of risk and the best possible return.

Why? Because we can control the business strategies. It's the ol' tortoise versus the hare way.

Historically, the most reliable way!

* * *

NINETEEN
CHEAP + CHEAP = ?

What's the number one strategy that never seems to work? Pay attention, penny watchers!

One day I came home and my father-in-law was there, a nice guy, but I was in a bad mood and I said to him, "You're pretty good at math, are you not?" He responded by saying, "Yes, I am."

So I asked him what "cheap plus cheap" equaled.

Now, not to pick on him because he's done a lot of great things, but he is known to be penny wise, if you get my drift. We've all heard the old expression originated by the 16th century philosopher Robert

Burton: "Penny wise, pound foolish." Or, as we say in America, dollar foolish. Although in China, it's "penny wise, *penny* foolish" because the word for penny is the same as the word for dollar, a.k.a yuan. (Is Don Yuan a Chinese womanizer? Asking for a friend.) But it's not about pinching pennies, is it? Nooo, it's not. It's about investing dollars or pounds (or yuans). Which, needless to say, is why we *all* can benefit from hiring a pro. Because without a pro it can be very difficult to build wealth. If it were easy, everyone would be rich. Of course, everyone *can* be rich. Which brings us back, once again, as to why we all can benefit from hiring a pro a.k.a. CFP® professional.

So— what causes humans to be cheap?

Penny-pinching?

Nope.

Fanny-pinching?

Of course not.

Emotions?

Hell, yes.

Is emotion a short term or long term thing?

It is short term.

Short like these sentences.

Don't get me wrong, saving money makes us feel good in the short term, too, but, as we know, not everything that feels good in the short term is good for us in the long term.

As Laura L. Cartensen, Director of the Stanford Center on Longevity, said, "Historically, humans didn't live long term."

This long-term thing is new! Maybe short-term emotional decisions are the enemy. This is why most people who "want it all *now*" don't stand a chance of becoming rich.

So, does this mean rich people are smarter? No!

One of my clients said it best when he said, "The reason I work for myself is because nobody else will hire me." That's also why immigrants are three and a half times more likely to become rich.

Say you are from Mexico, and don't have a great education. I'm sorry, but no corporation is going to hire you. Not a single one. So, what do you do? Yes, you should start your own business. Because who has the most money? Business owners, that's who. Which is why immigrants are three and a half times more likely to become richer than your sons, or my sons.

Holy cannoli!

But, getting back to penny wise—

If you're too cheap to hire people then, of course, you are greatly limited on how much you can make. (Because, like Emerson said, it's all about multiplying your presence.) Example: highest paid doctor compared to what Warren Buffet makes. Not even close.

Optimism can help, yes. And pessimism can have

a negative effect, true. This is why economics was invented.

Before economics, though, there was mercantilism, which spanned from the 16th century to the 18th century and was based on the principle that the world's wealth was static. You must take into mind, though, that only a dozen years prior, great minds thought the world was flat. The European nations that believed in mercantilism attempted to amass the largest imaginable share of the wealth by maximizing their exports and limiting their imports via tariffs. (Sound familiar?) But not till Adam Smith was there a methodical study of how economies worked. Mr. Smith, an 18th century Scotchman known by some as "The Father of Economics" and by others as "The Father of Capitalism," took some of the theories of French physiocrats—who believed that agriculture was the source of all wealth and its products, therefore, should be highly priced and stressed the necessity of free trade—and introduced economics, the science of how goods and services are produced and consumed, and how it was scarcity that drove economies. Leave it to the Scots. (I once made the acquaintance of someone who was part Scotch and part soda—but that's getting off topic.)

Most modern economic theories, however, are based on the work of Milton Friedman, a Nobel Prize Winner. Uncle Miltie was a firm believer that more capital in the system lessens the need for government involvement.

But, once again, I digress.

Emerson, as I mentioned earlier, wrote about this in his essay on compensation. He talked about working on the farm. As you recall, he said if he worked a day he could produce ten units of work. If he hires another worker, that's an additional ten units of work resulting in twenty units of work a day. Well, as I previously mentioned, he found out that this was completely wrong. The correct answer was that they produced thirty units of work.

So now you know why businesses make so much. And why multiplying your presence is key.

Also some pages back, I wrote about W. Edward Deming and how he offered to help the Detroit auto companies become more efficient, and how they said "no thank you, we're already making a ton of money" (or words to that effect) and how Mr. Deming took his ideas to Japan and how the rest is, as they say, history. Well, I think everyone running a business, big or small, should take note of something Mr. Deming wrote: "Nobody goes to work to mess things up."

You mean people go to work to do a good job?

Absobleepinglutely. That's why business owners and stockholders are able to do so well.

* * *

STEVE LYNCH

TWENTY

THINK YOU DON'T HAVE A CHANCE TO BE RICH?

If that's what you think, then you never will be.

They say seeing is believing. I say saving is believing. And the more you believe, baby, the richer you could become.

In 1982, Michael Jackson's "Thriller" was released, the 49ers won the Super Bowl, the NY Islanders won the Stanley Cup, Cardinals won the World Series, and Deep Purple came out with their Live In London album. It was also the year somebody shared a little game with me.

It went like this.

You have a choice, pick one:

You can have $1,000,000 today

- or -

You can have a penny that doubles every
day for one month.

Okay, what would you choose?

A million bucks in one fell swoop? Or one cent
doubling?

Well, if you took the doubling penny, in 31 days
you would've ended up with over $21,000,000. That
last sentence is deserving of an exclamation mark or
two. So here it is: *$21,000,000!!*

Now in 1982, I was twenty-two years old and this
did not impress me. I could not be stopped and had to
go for the big money. Sounds like "Fools Rush In?" Or
"The Tortoise and The Hare?"

More like "The Tortoise and the Hare*brained*."

P.T. Barnum said, "There's a sucker born every minute."

Well, I guess we're all suckers until we're not!

W.C. Fields said, "Never give a sucker an even break." Well, my little chickadee, I beg to differ. Everybody deserves a break. Because, like I said, we're all suckers until we're *not!*

Okay, let's continue the game. Ready for another one?

Someone twenty-five-years-old decides to invest for 35 years. Which is the smarter investment?

Investing $10,000 all at once?

- or -

Investing $250 a month?

Hypothetically, the $10,000 could have grown to $1,200,000. Not too shabby. However—the $250 a month could've doubled that! Grown to $2,400,000!*

Amazeballs!

Working in the financial planning biz for thirty-plus years, I have seen people hold out until they got a lump sum. The lump sum could, of course, be $10,000 or $50,000. Their *emotions* are impairing them. Do not let your emotions talk you out of sitting on that egg a little longer so it's fully hatched. We have clients of all ages that take advantage of this timeless investment strategy.

Now, of course, the best option may be doing both. Invest the $10,000, then, if you can, add $250 a month. But the most important thing is get cracking. Shake a leg. Don't wait! Time passes rapidly, and opportunity disappears quickly!

By the way, hypothetically, $3,700,000 is what investing $10,000 plus $250 a month over a time frame of 35 years comes out to.

Amazeballs, part II.

For the person asking "what investment did I use?" (Don't you mean what was the *widget* we used?)

Well, there were many different investments/widgets that could have accomplished this. Fortunately, my company (Steve Lynch Wealth Management) is unobstructed on investment choices, i.e., independent —what you should demand from whomever it is you get your guidance from. But, above all, don't let some get-rich-quick compulsion run amok!

We live in a free market enterprise. All you need is a plan! Because... YOU HAVE TO THINK PAST TOMORROW!

* * *

*A note regarding hypothetical investment results: hey are for illustrative purposes only. Calculations do not consider taxes, inflation, fees or other expenses.   his does not represent any specific product and should not be deemed a representation of past or future investment results. Actual investment results may be more or less than those shown.

TWENTY-ONE

STAIRWAY TO FINANCIAL HEAVEN.

As a kid, Led Zeppelin aside (although *their* "Stairway" has one of the greatest guitar solos of all time), at one point in my career (no, not as a guitarist) I used a stairway graphic to demonstrate the four or so steps your money ought to take. (I probably quit using the stairway graph when I started taking the elevator.) The stairway analogy is a simple and effective way of showing you that where you put your money (and *when*) doesn't have to get complicated. (I guess I borrowed it from the construction business, which I grew up in.) (Hey, what's with all these parentheses?)

(LOL)

Everyone wants to know the best places to put your money, at various stages. Well, here you go! (My apologies for the squiggly-ass way I draw but I'm a financial planner, not an architect, draftsman or Leonardo da Vinci.)

(Sheesh! There I go again making with the parentheses!)

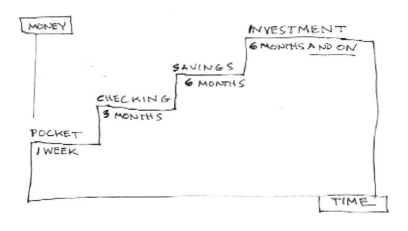

Pardon my mixing metaphors, but think of the steps as graduating from kindergarten to first grade, then to middle school, then high school, and finally college.

So step on up to the budgetary stairway diagram, but hold on to the bannister—which metaphorically is your CFP® professional—after all, we don't want you to miss a step, slip and fall down.

When you climb one step, move up to the next step, and so forth. There will be a skip in your step when you reach the top one. (But if you don't take the stairway approach, pain awaits.)

(There you go again, Steve, with the parentheses!)

So let's start with the bottom step. "Pocket."

Keep some money in your pocket in the likely event you'll need some. Like, let's say, you bump into Vito Corleone. He wants that sawbuck you've owed him since Super Bowl XV. He says he doesn't take Visa, just dough and the closest ATM is a mile away. So you reach into your pocket, pull out a crisp portrait of Alexander Hamilton and bada bing bada boom, Vito gives you a fist bump (instead of a fist to the solar plexus) and says "Have a great day, pal!" And saunters off. As for me, if I have $200 in my pocket, that's enough to cover one week.

Okay now, move on to the next step. "Checking."

Have enough to cover three months of expenditures. The rest goes into the next step.

Now, let's say you have money in your pocket (step one), then in checking (step two), then a 401(k). No good! You skipped a step!

That's right, you skipped putting money in a savings account. If you get into a jam but you put your money in a 401(k), you can't touch it without penalties.* This is where people get tripped up.

So the third step on the stairway is "Savings." I

---

*Although no blanket rules apply and some plans may make exceptions.

usually suggest building your savings for about six months. But, by all means, save!

Then it's on to the top step. "Investments."

Pretty simple, huh, Simon?

But, to make sure, I'll recap:

If you get $200, let's say, and you're going to use it within the week, then the best place to put this money is in your pocket. *Ka-ching!* (Oh wait, pockets don't *ka-ching.* Unless you're carrying in that pocket, along with money, a little talking parrot. *"Ka-ching!* Polly wants a retirement plan, *awk!"*)

Then you have your "monthly bills" money. Best place for that is in your checking account. After a while, you know how much works best for you.

Then next step would be a savings account and maybe an emergency money fund. A money market works fine.

The next step after that would be to start some

investments for the long term. Stocks, well diversified. And, most importantly, adding to this every month. I'm sure you get the idea.

But I must, once again, emphasize: do not skip any steps on the stairway. For example, you have money in a checking account and someone in payroll, let's say, routinely puts a little something in the 401(k). So you move from the second step to the fourth step. So now, uh-oh, a big portion of your money cannot be touched until you're fifty-nine-and-a-half-freaking-years-old. That means if you need something, you'll probably have to dive headfirst into your credit cards. The average couple has around $16,000 in credit card bills. I hate to think of the interest they are paying. Which is why I think they push the 401(k) snare waaaay too hard.

At any rate, the stairway is a simple way to work your money. And "simple" has many benefits. Right, Polly?

"Awk! Ka-ching!"

(No parentheses or parrots were harmed in the making of this chapter.)

* * *

STEVE LYNCH

TWENTY-TWO
THE G WORD

"It's a cinch!"

You've heard that expression, right? Of course you have.

"Is Kiss My Bupkis gonna win The Derby?" asks some working stiff neophyte.

"It's a cinch!" replies some confidence-man, licking his chops. He eats neophytes for breakfast.

You get the picture.

Well, fundamentally, that's what someone is saying when they say something is guaranteed. (Yes, that's the

G Word.)

But, of course, nothing in actuality is guaranteed. No horserace result. No investment outcome. In life, the only thing guaranteed is death, taxes and stubbing your toe in the middle of the night. Okay, I admit that stubbing your toe, even though I do it way too often, is not fully guaranteed.

The word "guaranteed", and where and how it's used, I've always found disconcerting, to say the least. Why? Well, like I said, where in nature is anything guaranteed? Nowhere, that's where! (Except for, like I said, death, taxes and the occasional broken toe.)

So is it a real word? We know "cinch" is a real word. It's the strap that holds a saddle on a horse. Does it guarantee that the saddle won't come lose? Hell, no. But it's the best assurance any equestrian has. Aside from maybe Krazy Gluing your rump to the horse's. And even that's iffy.

So, is a guarantee something contrived by conmen to sell you stuff? Is it just a bill of goods? A snow job? A bucket of bullshit? I have always tried to educate my clients. Meaning, show them the ins and outs of every investment. I guess what I'm saying is, guarantees are, by and large, fabrications, mendacities, deceptions, big fat lies.

If you're licensed in securities—meaning to trade stocks (buy or sell)—the "securities police" would lock you up and throw away the key if you used the word guaranteed. The G Word is a no-no.

Now, if you have a life insurance company with annuities and life insurance that the company guarantees (income, death benefit, etc.), then so mehow they get to use the G Word — but only if they include the appropriate disclosure..

So—where's the problem, Mr. Steve "Holier Than Thou" Lynch? What irks me is "guaranteed" means to the insurance company that, *while they are in business*, they will abide by the guarantee. Now, from the clients' standpoint, they like the G Word because the stock market is too volatile. So slap on a guarantee and breathe a sigh of relief? It don't work that way, Chester. Because here's the catch: if what you are worried about happens, namely the stock markets goes down and never gets back up is that insurance company still in business? The answer is probably no. So what about your guarantee, Jethro? It goes up in smoke, that's what it does. Like a Cheech and Chong spiff. Poof!

What about that bank's guarantee? You know, the one that the US Government stands behind? Well, Maribel, what they guarantee is your deposit. So if you deposit a hundred bucks, they guarantee you a hundred bucks. But not any interest that you might've earned. And if not for the interest you might as well have hid that money in your mattress.

So the point is, do you have "stock market" risk by putting your money in a bank? The answer is no, except if the market collapses then your silly piece of paper will not buy anything. But many still are persuaded by that non-word word: guaranteed.

Look, you know me, Al— I speak straight from the shoulder (Mr. Bluebird's favorite perch, zip-a-dee-doo-dah and all that) and I think we would all be a lot better off if we stopped looking for free shit. That is another word that has no meaning in Nature. There's no such thing as a free lunch, and all that jazz, yada yada! The answer is always: *Have a plan, man.*

Most people deal with one-dimensional salesmen. Not an independent CFP® professional that's using long term (hopefully) non-emotional (definitely) decision making.

That's the ticket!

That's economics, baby! Or, as Mr. Bluebird

would say, "It's the truth, it's actch'll, everything is satisfactch'll!"

* * *

TWENTY-THREE

THE NAME OF THE GAME
Optimal return with minimal risk

In the short term, it's difficult to see the upshot of an emotional decision. We're caught up in the heat of the moment. In the long term, of course, blunders are clearly apparent. We try, nonetheless, to justify an emotional decision that went awry with some kind of logic. Or at least we try. But it's true what they say about hindsight, that it's 20/20. Or like Bob Dylan said, "you don't need a weatherman to know which way the wind blows." But when it comes to money, you do need a trusted adviser. Someone who's not making emotional decisions. Instead of thinking with the heart, an experienced planner is using his noodle. Think of it as two modes of thought. One is thinking fast, thinking on your feet, thinking *emotionally*—which can be reckless or, more times than not, stupid. The other mode of thought is slower, more deliberative, more logical, more commonsensical, using forethought— keeping emotions at bay.

Emotional decisions can lead you astray. From "it's just one chocolate donut covered with rainbow sprinkles, it ain't gonna make me a tub of lard" to "I don't need to invest for the future."

But the truth is, thinking in the long-term is like: "Okay, that donut was damn good, but if I eat a dozen more it'll probably go straight to my ass!"

Hopefully, my writing this book makes you realize just how easy it can be to get rich. Seriously, what if the road to riches was simply the act of investing for the future? And never losing hope! As a matter of fact, under the glass furniture protector on my desk I have the following maxim:

Three Grand Essentials To Happiness:

1. Something to DO.

2. Something to LOVE.

3. Something to HOPE for.

Oh sure, some people will say, "Hell, Steve, I'm too old to start investing." But if you recall, my friend Jimmy was investing just fifty bucks a month and, when he began, he was certainly no spring chicken. More like an autumn chicken. And when it came to hope, he never lost it and is, today, a wealthy man.

Yes, everyone can have hope. Can having hope make you live longer? I bet this has already been proven. I know someone who once wrote a joke or two for Bob Hope and he told me that never was someone so aptly named, maybe that's why Hope lived a hundred years. (And I'm sure many a wise investment somehow contributed to his long life.)

If it's the journey and not the trophy, then maybe we all should never retire. Maybe we should all keep building because that's what gives us the feeling of expressing ourselves fully! This is one of the greatest joys there is. And how many people miss out? Remember, Jimmy just did $50 a month.

One morning I woke up with an idea. This, before my first cup of coffee: nobody gets rid of a bad habit—they get a new habit to replace it.

So I called Dr. Al, my client, and he said I was correct.

I think saving is a good habit that abolishes many bad habits.

During World War II, Dr. Al escaped from Lithuania with his mother and sister. Sadly, his father was never seen again. But Dr. Al never let go of hope and became a "head doctor" and my client for thirty-plus years.

Hope is good!

* * *

TWENTY-FOUR

THE WIDGET MISCONCEPTION

S tarring Steve Lynch. Not to be confused with Gidget starring Sandra Dee. True, Sandra Dee was cuter than me. (My wife would disagree, though—or, at least, let's hope so.) But I ask you, who has more fun? Blondes? Or CERTIFIED FINANCIAL PLANNERS™ professional? Well, I can only speak for myself (a blonde with a scattering of gray) when I say a CFP® professional has lots of fun—because it's fun helping clients grow wealth.

You may be asking yourself, "Whoa, Steve! Where are you headed with this?" The misconception about widgets, that's where I'm headed. A widget, as you now know, is a term used in business and business schools to describe a Product. Instead of calling it a hammer or a Corvette, or a computer, or a Pet Rock, in business they call it a widget. We were all led to believe that to get rich you had to invent one. But the fact of the matter is, most rich people—98.5%, to be exact—never invented a widget. So it's not the widget that makes an investment a viable, valuable one, it's the *business*.

In college, as I mentioned earlier, I got the ol' widget itch and came up with another way to dig underground horizontally using water and an air pump. A bank, the state of New Mexico and New Mexico State University all wanted to get involved. Oh man, I thought I'd struck it rich. Luckily, I got shares and went back to college.

I had inventor blood in me, as my mom would say, but I started to think! Can a person make money without inventing something?

No need to reinvent the wheel because that's not where the money is.

It's about the business, not the widget. But this is how "amateurs" try to do it with a widget—hope for the get-rich-quick unicorn—until they wake up, like I did.

Think the tortoise and the hare. Steady and sure wins the race.

What about retirement plans? They, too, are the widget. But keep in mind, a lot of retirement plans have failed. When you look from the client's side even 401(k) plans are far from perfect. But, of course, when they do work, you still don't have a plan to "mind your own business." After all, business-minded people are the ones who end up with the most. It's true now as it was a thousand years ago.

The pro's (hopefully) know that concentrating on

the widgets is only a small part of the total formula. It doesn't need to be sexy, because the goal is to get the best return with the least amount of risk. That is financial planning, that is business. And most everyone is doing their financial planning all wrong. They think how a person gets rich is by being extraordinary or having amazing talent. It certainly doesn't hurt. But the truth is, like I said, 98.5% did business. This is why I say anybody can get rich. There is no shortage of money. Maybe this is why yours truly is on his high horse trying to spread the word. I'm glad I'm not chasing widgets anymore. The real rainbow—the real unicorn—is minding your business, baby. Now giddy-up.

* * *

TWENTY-FIVE

RISK. HOW TO BETTER UNDERSTAND IT

Everything you do has elements at risk. Taking a selfie while driving, for example. Or moving in with the in-laws—which is akin to living at the foot of a volcano. Risk rhymes with tsk-tsk. Like buying blowfish from a gas station cooler. Holding a golf club above your head during a thunderstorm. Having a pet tsetse fly. Or maybe simply kicking back with a six-pack watching your favorite show, thinking life is a bowl of Munchos, while, unbeknownst to you, that retirement plan at the office has turned out to be punier than Barney Fife.

What I'm saying is, there is risk everywhere. No matter what you're doing, or whether you're doing nothing at all. There it is, at every turn and in all directions. Risk! Here, there, everywhere (as The Beatles sang). Every which way—whether it's high or low, far or wide, there's risk, risk, RISK!

Oh well, enough of the dramatics, I think you get the idea.

There. Is. Risk. End of story.

Which brings us to the topic at hand, which is understanding it. Because the more you understand, the more you can reduce it.

For example, one Sunday (and by one, I mean one since I don't go over to my in-laws all that much) I'm talking to my stepfather-in-law, Barney. Nice guy, retired from a national laboratory and is also a physicist. So he's no dummy. He started in the 1950's, the Eisenhower administration. I asked him if a person went to school for 29 years, got all A+'s, out of all the knowledge in all the universities, how much knowledge could one person gain. Well, Barney started talking about gigabytes—which is a unit of information equal to one billion (10^9) or, strictly, 2^{30} bytes. (I threw the mathematics in simply to showoff. After all, I *am* a CFP® professional.). After a while he said the amount of knowledge one person could possibly obtain is about a 100th of 1% of all the knowledge out there. That means we don't know much! So how do we live? So how do we make decisions? Simple. We base it on history. As they say, 99% of the stuff we worry about never happens. Helen Keller, the first deaf-blind person to earn a Bachelor of Arts degree, said, "Security is mostly a superstition. It does not exist in nature. Avoiding danger is no safer in the long run than outright exposure. Life is either a daring adventure, or nothing." Humankind has achieved real greatness. Accomplishments that are truly amazing. But there are periods in our history that are down right horrific. And the story, at least thus far, has always ended the same way. We, humans, despite all our flaws, and in spite of the fact that we can only retain 0.01% of knowledge, we somehow, some way manage to move on to even greater feats. Greater heights—and, yes, greater knowledge. Furthermore, believe it or, we continue to get smarter and smarter! (Unless you're among those who are getting dumber and dumber. But, considering you're reading this book, I seriously doubt it.)

There are simple ways to reduce risk.

Don't make emotional decisions, which is almost impossible. It's also why you hire a CERTIFIED FINANCIAL PLANNER™ professional. He or she is not emotional about your situation. Cooler heads prevail. So do educated ones.

I have always heard more people have lost money trying not to lose money. Which also goes with: I've seen the enemy, and the enemy is us.

Lastly, conmen use fear as their magic. Don't ever let anyone frighten you into a decision. As FDR said as he led America out of a Great Depression, "Fear nothing but fear itself." (Unless you're a quarterback, and then most definitely fear those swift, gigantic pass rushers.)

So remember Helen Keller's brave words of wisdom. Or Ralph Waldo Emerson's "Fear defeats more people than any other thing." Or, with my apologies to Rudyard Kipling, "If you can keep your head, when all about you are losing theirs, chances are you have a coolheaded CERTIFIED FINANCIAL PLANNER.™ professional"

Yep, it *pays* to be cool!

* * *

TWENTY-SIX
STUPID TAX VERSUS SMART TAX

 W ithout a CFP® professional, life can be very taxing.

If you jumped into a time machine and asked one of our Founding Fathers—Sam Adams, for example— what he considered a stupid tax, he probably would've said the tax on tea. And you know where that tax led us. (Hint: "*One*, if by *land*, and *two*, if by *sea!*") Back then, tea was second only to water as The Colonies most consumed beverage; a more popular drink than even the one brewed with Sam Adam's famous malted barley. Imagine if the British Parliament had taxed something less beloved by the colonists, like a

Tall Non-Fat Latte Grande With Caramel Drizzle, would there ever have been an American Revolution? (Fortunately, Starbucks wasn't around back then.)

But, getting back to the title of this chapter—

There is a smart tax and there is a stupid tax. The overriding point is to do everything you can to get to the smart tax. The stupid tax, of course, should be avoided at all costs. But, let's face it, the Average Joe and Average Josephine rarely know how to avoid it. We have all paid our share of the stupid tax but that doesn't mean we shouldn't have a plan—a *financial* plan—to get where we are only paying the smart tax. The first step is identifying the problem. Once you do, then you, too, can save.

Let's start with the stupid tax. This is for people that have ordinary income, which we all either have or had. You work at Wendy's, let's say, and you make an income that is taxed at the ordinary tax rate which for 2020 varies from 10% to 37% depending on your amount of ordinary income. Yes, you got it: 37% if you're successful. So, how many of you out there want to pay 37% in federal tax? Raise your hand (or wave a white flag). Probably not very many, right? Oh, wait, I forgot to add in the state tax, too. Now I call this stupid because anybody in his or her right mind is going to try to avoid paying that much tax. You can either stop working as hard as you are and earn less or contribute to a retirement plan. But wait a minute! You'll still have to pay the stupid tax on the backend. (That's right, when you take the money out). Not good. Not smart.

A smart tax maxes out at 20% in addition to state tax. As of 2021, if you make less than $501,600 your tax rate would be 15%. Nice! And if you make less than $80,800 the tax rate is 0%. Super nice![2]

One morning I woke up with this picture in my

head. No, it wasn't a picture of pancakes and bacon. It was an amusement park. Like the one my big sister (and big brother) worked at. One day, Amy, my sister, took me there and, oh my! For a ten-year-old kid like myself, the sounds and smells of an amusement park was pure nirvana. (By the way, she also took me to my first concert! Sure, she was "babysitting" me, but, still, how many little kids ever got to see the great Mitch Ryder and The Detroit Wheels!) But I digress. Here's the smart tax versus stupid tax "picture" I had in my head when I woke up the morning after the amusement park experience:

When you get off one ride, you're sick. Like, let's say, "Tilt-a-Whirl." If you're like ten-year-old me, you focused on the center of the cart you're seated in, which doesn't move. The mind thinks it sees something motionless while the body is whipped with quick twists and turns which sends a mixed signal to the brain, which in turn is likely to trigger motion sickness and other horrors. (The only Vertigo I ever liked was the one starring Kim Novak.) But when you get off of the other ride, the one that makes you happy, not sick, like the Sky Diver, you're exhilarated. So I ask you, which "tax ride" are you getting on? The one that makes you feel elated or the one that makes you puke?

I once heard a saying that went like this: "You don't know if something is good until ten years after." Well, I don't know if you have to wait *that* long, but knowing the start, the midpoint and, of course, what will happen when you take money out is what we all should do. Oh, and also what happens to the 401(k) investment if one croaks? That's right, *more* taxes! Seriously, you deserve better. You deserve a smarter tax.

The one area of consensus is that the most pro-growth policies are those that improve incentives to work, save, invest, and innovate. The US government wants to take advantage of this because if you invest in a company (own stocks in said company) you are helping that company, which in turn helps everyone. The US government is not dumb. People that invest allow companies more resources to build new factories and, of course, hire more workers. Shazam! Better jobs, more taxes—a win/win/win.

One way of building a good financial plan would be to work in reverse. Where you want to finish lets you know where to start. And where you want to be down the road is at the smart tax. With financial planning, you move in that direction. Because smart *is* what smart *does*.

* * *

---

[2] Please note that our discussion of the "stupid tax" refers to ordinary income taxes, and "smart tax" refers to the capital gains tax that applies to investments. However, please consult with your tax professional as we do not provide tax or legal advice.

TWENTY-SEVEN

FIND THE PONY!
(The key to dealing with bad times.)

Just remember we came into this world with nothing, zilch, zip—not even a pot to piddle in. Or, for that matter, a diaper. And when we leave this world we can't take anything with us. Not a nickel. Not a sausage. But while we're here there are good times and bad times. But without bad times, there would be no reason to work to make things better. At least, to my knowledge. For example, in 1987 I moved to Albuquerque, New Mexico. Two months later, the stock market went kerplop! It had the largest one-day drop in history—or, at least, up until then. (Not till March 2020 would there be a larger drop.) But my point is this, dear reader: I have lived and run a financial planning business through at least five hellish market crashes— kerplop, kerplop, kerplop, kerplop, kerplop! And since the beginning of time, there has been one consistent event: mankind has always pulled through. 100% recovered.

There are two kinds of people in this world: the pessimist and the optimist. Ronald Reagan, a famous optimist, relished telling a certain tale about a cheery child and his custodian who, as a punishment for no particular reason other than schadenfreude, locked the small boy in a windowless room full of horse manure. (Reagan always kept his stories clean—at least, in public.) After twenty minutes or so, the ogre opened the door expecting the child's good nature to be shattered and couldn't believe what he saw. The boy—in high spirits, a big grin on his face—was enthusiastically rummaging through the disgusting heap of manure.

"What the hell are you doing?" screamed the heartless custodian.

"With all this manure," exclaimed the chipper child gleefully, "there must be a PONY in here somewhere!"

So, *yes*— when times are shitty, look for the pony!

Which brings up another topic I'm passionate about...

We all have free will, use it!

Free will—not to be confused with *Free Willy*, a fair-to-middling children's film—is the freedom of choice and the power of self-determination. The great writer Jim Harrison wrote: "Secret desires remain weak fantasies unless they pervade a *will* strong enough to carry them out." (The stick-to-itiveness I stated earlier in the book.)

One of my clients called and was nervous about the stock market. I said this does not change your plan. This particular client owns a machine shop. So I said something that would shake him to his core. "If you bought a milling machines for $100,000," I said, "and someone offered you $10,000 for them, would you sell?" And, of course, he said: "Hell no!"

Your stocks are the same. If you don't sell, you still have the same amount of assets as you did before the stock market turmoil. Don't be suckered into selling. In stressful times when people get hurt it's generally by their own doing.

What's more, watching the market can drive a person batty. But remember, we live in the greatest country. And owning stock in the companies that contribute to our country's greatness is— well, effing great! But when the market hits a little turbulence, what are you going to do? Bail? What do you do when your flight hits a few bumps? You don't open

the overwing exit and leap 30,000 feet! Of course not,

pilgrim, you order your third Chardonnay, is what

you do. I never recommend running from a bear or a

bearish market. That's a sure way to get bit in the ass.

My advice? Find the pony!

* * *

TWENTY-EIGHT

SMART VERSUS SOPHISTICATED

It's good to be king. But believe me when I say it's even better to be smart. But what good is it being smart if you lack sophistication? By sophisticated I don't necessarily mean someone with cultivated tastes in, let's say, Neoclassic art, or Napoleon Cognac, or Wagnerian arias. (Although it would be cool to see the lead singer for Twisted Sister in the role of Brunhilda.) Sure, it's chic to be cultured but so is yogurt. By being sophisticated, monetarily-speaking, I'm referring to someone with the worldly experience (and business acumen) to seek the advice of experts. It would be naïve not to, and not the least sophisticated.

I'm reminded of the saying: "Self-sufficiency is the road to poverty." And don't forget what Edward Deming said about everyone goes to work to do a good job. So, if you don't multiply your presence (thank you, Ralph Waldo Emerson) then you'll, more than likely, be put out of existence.

A sophisticated military general, for example, seeks the advice of military intelligence. Your seeking the advice of a CERTIFIED FINANCIAL PLANNER™ professional is both sophisticated and pretty damn smart.

I rest my case, General.

* * *

TWENTY-NINE
TOUGH LOVE

Don't ask me why I have a chapter on tough love. Maybe it's because that's how I was raised. Or maybe, when it comes to expressing adoration, I lack that lovey-dovey, mushy-gushy chromosome. I try my best, of course, to express it the best way that I can. Like trying to make my clients rich. Or my kids walk the straight and narrow. What's more, I never forget anniversaries or birthdays.

Well, hardly ever.

Yet, for me, there is but one love—and that's *tough* love. Am I right, Coach Belichick? I suppose one rational is because I have one of those tell-it-like-it-is, no-nonsense "logistician" personalities. Logic—like bacon—goes great with just about everything. I prefer numbers to words. (Hell, if I could've written this book using numerals instead of an alphabet, I would've—but that would've taken way 2 much cre8tivity.)

Oh, don't get the wrong idea, I'm not a cold fish. And I can schmooze with the best of them. I just don't like to bullshit. I try to tell it like it is—hopefully, without offending too many. (Emphasis on *hopefully*.)

So, whether I'm on the court showing my kids how to ace a serve, or in the office advising a client how to achieve his or her long-term financial goal, I pull few punches. I'm a proponent of tough love.

* * *

THIRTY

SYMPATHY VERSUS EMPATHY

Building wealth has a very large emotional side to it and it helps to know the difference between sympathy and empathy.

Sympathy is feeling sorrowful about someone's misfortune.

Empathy is the ability to understand people's feelings as if we were having the same exact feelings ourselves! Empathy goes beyond sympathy. It's to project your imagination so you actually feel what the other person is feeling. Put yourself in the other person's place. Walk a mile in his shoes.

It's the difference between feeling *for* someone and feeling *with* someone.

Sympathy is giving unsolicited advice.

Empathy is listening and, if asked, giving sound advice. So I guess you can say I'm one empathetic son of a gun.

* * *

STEVE LYNCH

THIRTY-ONE

THE THIRD BEST INVESTMENT

Okay, before we get to the third best investment, let's get the first two "best investments" out of the way.

Drum roll, please…

The first "best investment" is making yourself smarter.

Whatever it takes. Continue your schooling, keep reading, ask questions… and listen to experts.

The second "best investment" is making yourself healthier.

For starters: eating right, getting enough sleep, reducing use of alcohol and tobacco, take plenty of exercise… and a willingness to listen to experts.

Quick recap, thus far:

(1) Invest in making yourself smarter. ✔

(2) Invest in making yourself healthier. ✔

So far, sounds easy, right? Easier said than done. Start with baby steps and you'll be fine. And now, on to the third "best investment."

Is it land? After all, land used to be fought over so it must be the third "best investment." That might have been true once upon a time, so people could farm the land—everything from potatoes to petunias. Is the third "best investment" oil? In my conference room I have a globe which, now and then, I like to spin—occasionally getting my fingers caught in it like Inspector Clouseau, and it hurts like hell. But looking at this globe (when it's not spinning) sums things up rather quickly. For example, on this basketball-size sphere, Russia is about the size of a large T-bone steak and has plenty of land and oil. Then compare Russia with, let's say, the size of Japan—which, in comparison, looks like a teeny seahorse. You can place about forty-five "Japans" inside the Russian borders. (If you were to say that one of the motives of Imperial Japan in WWII was to expand its territory, you'd in all probability be right.) Yet, today, the economy of Japan has grown to be three times greater than Russia's. So I suppose we can eliminate the importance of land and oil—not to mention size.

Okay, so where am I going with this? The *third* "best investment"—*that's* where. People have been trying to figure this one out for eons. So here it is: number three on the Investments Hit Parade is— (another drum roll, please)—brainpower! Or, in many cases, investing in someone else's. (Yes, an expert's.)

The human intelligence when unleashed is the most powerful force in the universe. But did you know that a mastery of situations can actually make us smarter as we get older? According to *Psychological Science*, researchers report that across a hundred days of testing people sixty-five and over showed less erraticism in their cognitive performance than did younger people aged twenty to thirty-one. This fascinated me. Because you'd think it would be the opposite, right? You know, younger minds would have less variability. But such is not the case. That's because a mature adult's greater consistency is due to "learned strategies to solve the task, a constantly high motivation level, as well as a balanced daily routine and stable mood." Who would've thunk? But get this: I think one of the easiest advantage of mature adults is *buying stocks*. And using the brainpower of an expert— namely a CFP® professional.

Now don't get me wrong, no investment is perfect. The stock market has a thermometer stuck in its ear which scares the you-know-what out of most beginners. The more-experienced investor, however, knows that everything is moving; changing constantly. Just because nobody is telling me what the value of my house is doesn't mean it isn't changing. Corporations (and its stocks) are the engine that powers all economies. The better the businesses, the better the country. And because we're a country that harnesses its brainpower, the end result is we have some of the greatest companies in the world.

Lastly (which, fittingly, rhymes with ghastly), there are some people who like to put down Wall Street, or at least try to. But without Wall Street and its companies, wouldn't most of us be unemployed? What's more, the heart of Wall Street, as I mentioned previously, is not in New York. That's just where they keep score, so to speak. The heart of Wall Street is on every street, in every town, in every state in the country—and beyond!

Okay, before I step down from my soapbox, I need to make one more point: The whole system is designed for the benefit of the average person, not just Rich Uncle Pennybags. (That portly old guy with a white moustache wearing a top hat in the game of Monopoly.) In fact, you don't even have to look rich to be rich. Just a willingness to listen to experts. You do that and you don't need the top hat, you can walk around all day in your boxer shorts.

* * *

STEVE LYNCH

THIRTY-TWO

IF YOU CHEAT, YOU CHEAT YOURSELF

This, one of my favorite sayings, I snatched—I mean, *borrowed*—from Ralph Waldo Emerson:

In labor as in life there can be no cheating. The thief steals from himself. The swindler swindles himself.

Or, as the great W.C. Fields once said, "You can't cheat an honest man."

For some, though, cheating feels like the best way (maybe the *only* way) to get ahead. Like the student who rolled up his sleeves during a test for the answers written on his arms. Would you feel confident in the hands of, let's say, a surgeon who cheated his way through med school? Hell, no! How about those elite athletes who ended up cheating only themselves and, subsequently, screwing up their lives by taking performance enhancing drugs. Studies show that dishonest behavior can take a toll on your well-being. (Yes, it's true: cheaters actually cheat themselves out of happiness.) And the tabloids, as you know, are teeming with celebrities cheating on their spouses. And business leaders participating in financial crimes.

Talk about cheating yourself, how about those who spend their hard-earned dough on the lotto? If you think you're going to strike it rich overnight by playing the lotto, you've got another think coming. The odds of winning the mega jackpot, for instance, is 1 in 302,575,350! Uh-huh, that's right, you heard me, booby. The odds of winning is *one* in almost *three-hundred-and-three-million!* Look at it this way, the odds of getting struck by lighting in just a one year period is 1 in 700,000. Which means, you'll get struck by lightning 432 times *before* you win one stupid lotto. 302,575,349 out of 302,575,350 is a hell of a lot of losers that could've been winners *if,* instead of throwing money away on a snowball's chance in hell, they did what Jimmy did. (Yeah, that same Jimmy who had me invest his monthly $50.) Like Jimmy, they could wind up, thus far, with $200,000! Now imagine if they had invested $500 a month, they could have $2,000,000! Yes, a whopping two mil. No ping pong balls or scratch card required. Just good old fashioned common sense.

Time is a key factor in a person's wealth creation. In fact, you might say *time* is the most precious asset that any of us have. You think I play the lottery? No way, Jose! Getting rich the slow way is the *surest* way to go.

So by not investing monthly, by spending precious time on unprofitable behaviors, people are cheating themselves. Big-time.

Here's another checklist for you:

- Patience is a sign of intelligence. ✔

- Wealthy people are typically patient people. ✔

- Think like the tortoise, not like the hare. ✔

- Think "Jimmy" as opposed to get-rich-quick ✔
  shit.

And, remember: deal only with professionals with a strong moral compass. Because, let's face it, if someone will cheat with you, they'll undoubtedly cheat *on* you. A CERTIFIED FINANCIAL PLANNER™ professional (such as *moi*) is a fiduciary—a person who is expected to act on behalf of another person, putting their clients' interest ahead of their own, someone bound both legally and ethically to act in the other's best interests, with a vow to preserve good faith and trust.

Which is why I recommend, along with following your conscience, letting a CERTIFIED FINANCIAL

PLANNER™ professional be your guide.

* * *

STEVE LYNCH

THIRTY-THREE

THE HUMAN GOAL THAT CAN NEVER BE REACHED.

("Y" people are richer)

Let's begin this little chapter with a million-dollar idea. Literally.

Daniel Kahneman, a behavioral economist known for his work on the psychology of judgment and decision-making, is a Nobel Laureate for challenging an old economics behavioral theory. And, as you may already know, a Nobel prize-winner is awarded a million bucks. Not bad, eh? A million simoleons for an idea!

Just think about it.

I did.

Like all inventors, we take an idea and build on it. And then cross-train the idea to use in a totally different arena.

So, here we go!

Economics is the study of how people make decisions.

Behavior Economics is a better understanding of economics.

Economists used to say humans (that's us—well, most of us) make decisions to maximize our wealth and our enjoyment. It was all about the profits. It was all about the numbers (equations, math, yada yada).

Then in walks Daniel Kahneman!

He says, "Yo! I would like to see the formula of love." (Actually, he didn't say "yo" but would've been cool if he had.) Anyway, The Holy Grail is the "Y" in the road. (Fear not, dear readers, I shall explain shortly.) Economists have been trying to predict which way people will go, right or left? And, of course, if you can predict which way people will go, you could really help society—not to mention, make a shitload of money.

Yup, like I said, The Holy Grail.

Daniel Kahneman is a Behavior Economist. And his million dollar idea is this (ha! you probably thought I'd never get around to it): Losing has such a larger effect on people than winning that all of the human species (I bet all species) will do anything to avoid losing. Coaches have used the saying "The best defense is a good offense." Which is true, unless in rare occasions when some flame-throwing pitcher tosses a no-hitter. Or some defensive lineman closely resembling The Hulk continuously sacks the quarterback.

But back to the "Y" … and "Y" (some) people tend to be richer. It's basically a contest between those who want to be Less Poor (LP) versus those who want to be

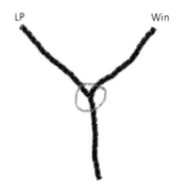

Winners (Win).

FYI: As a CERTIFIED FINANCIAL PLANNER™ professional that studied Economics in college, I use this Nobel Prize-winning wisdom for my client's benefit. With a dab of humor tossed in.

And, yes, a dollar equals a worker, an asset. Or to put it another way: $ = 🧍

The letter Y has a leg (the lower stroke is what it's called) and two arms (the upper strokes). Now imagine your assets are marching up your leg (ooh, that tickles!) until, holy moly, it gets to the proverbial fork in the road (or, in this case, the upper strokes of the

"Y"). Do you go left or right?

If you go left, your goal is to be nothing more than simply less poor (LP), which is what Kahneman says we're all doing because it's an innate characteristic; a behavior we're born with. Therefore, the goal of the left arm of the "Y" is to be less poor (LP), less chance of being embarrassed by being a LOSER.

Now, the right arm of the "Y" is a whole different ballgame with a whole different outcome. It's allocating our assets to win, baby, WIN. Or, to put it more succinctly, become wealthy. And then *more wealthy*.

See how the two arms (or strokes) are completely different? Less Poor versus More Wealth! Sounds really simple, does it not?

Okay, so what do I mean by "the human goal that can never be reached?"

As a person who will do anything to avoid being

a LOSER, we all march to the same drum, which is working our butts off (which is good) to march up the left arm (to pay off our bills and be less poor).

Now here's the billion-dollar question: can you ever pay off all your bills?

Well, let's look at it introspectively. If a person has a two hundred thousand or two hundred million debt (whatever the person's debt is) and that person works very, very hard because you can (I believe in you) and pays their debt down—heck, let's say you pay it *off*—the question, then, is: At this point how much money do you have? Answer: zero, of course.

So, then you go out and borrow more. Which brings us to the title of this little chapter: The Human Goal That Can Never Be Reached. Which is also a good place to remind you of Albert Einstein's definition of insanity: "Doing the same thing over and over again and expecting different results."

People are racing in the wrong direction. They're choosing to be LP's, not Winners. People suffer from being headstrong. (My dad used to say, "Boy, pull in your horns!") Anyway, you buy a house. You work very hard to pay it off. You find that the bills don't go away. Then you are too old to change. No money for a new roof and other essential home maintenance. After paying everything off, nobody has any money left. It might be why old neighborhoods get old. It's a sad tale. Which is why I'm always harping on setting up a savings investment plan. No matter how small. Because, as I'm somewhat renowned for saying, and I can't say it nearly enough: "Think big, start small." And hopefully, one day, someone will ask you why you're glowing, and you can say that your wealth is growing.

Like I said at the beginning of this book, everybody can be rich. And now that you've read this little book with its little steps, I hope you're well on your way.

* * *

STEVE LYNCH

THIRTY-FOUR
WHAT A WONDERFUL WORLD
(An epilogue, of sorts)

You know we all want just about the same thing. Basically, it's to be happy. Well, what does that mean? Allow me to paint a picture, see if you agree.

How about walking around the earth with an endless card that works just like money? How about having all your bills paid? Your only job is to have fun. Sounds too good to be true? Whether you believe it or not, there are people who, as we speak, are living this life. And a number of them are clients. This is my mission for them: A full concierge financial planning service. Pretty cool, eh?

Now, here is the sad part. If you are a *do-it-yourself,* *don't-trust-anyone-else* kind of person, then you will most likely never reach this point! That's why I wrote this book, *Mind Your Own Business.* To accomplish great things in this world, you can't be spending your time on things that don't interest you or give you enjoyment. What if Einstein spent his time mowing lawns or shoveling manure? I truly enjoy figuring out ways to make people rich. I go on vacation and talk to people about it. I think about it in my sleep. I always ask myself why didn't my father, who had a scholarship in Latin, go to college, discover gravity? The short answer is that he was always too busy working to ever sit under a tree and drink wine. I bet my father wasn't the only one.

Look, by many estimates, 80% of your success or profit comes from the planning. That's why planners get a master's degree or, more importantly, an MBA. Because, let's face it, there is no "degree" in widgeting.

The way I see it, your success, plain and simple, is 20% from the investment and 80% from the planning. Holy cow! I think I've driven home my point! Think big, start small. But act like a business, have a smart (and personalized) financial plan.

It's your chance to be happy.

A chance to mind your own business.

* * *

STEVE LYNCH

ABOUT THE AUTHOR

Stephen C. Lynch was born just outside of Detroit in Royal Oak, MI. He was the son of a WW II Veteran and an English major mom (may she overlook an occasional lapse in his vocabulary). From an early age, Steve tagged along with his father as he helped rebuild homes. It was then that he learned about saving money. That passion still exists through today. Yes, he loves to save money, but he also gets a kick out of dirt biking and mountain biking, and—oh yes—tennis. But his number one escape is fishing. He is married to Heidi and has four children (Kyle, Gavin, Megan, and Morgan). He's currently fostering an armadillo he affectionately named Ralph Waldo Emerson

Steve invites readers to email him at steve@stevelynchwealth.com.

STEVE LYNCH

A SPECIAL THANKS TO

Jesus Alvarez and Edwin Heaven, your encouragement and insistence was greatly appreciated.

And to the hundreds of clients and their families for trusting me with something as important as their future, I thank you kindly.

~ S.L